CONVERSATIONS THAT SELL

for

FINANCIAL ADVISORS

Communicate • Collaborate • Convert

CONVERSATIONS THAT SELL

for

FINANCIAL ADVISORS

Nancy Bleeke Noël

CONTENTS

The Wrap-Up

ACKNOWLEDGMENTS

I am blessed. My life and career are full of people who support and challenge me, create learning and growth opportunities for me, and celebrate with me. If not for them, I'd never have tackled writing another book!

First, heaps of admiration for the advisors with whom I am deeply honored to work with each day. Thank you to every one of you. Our work inspires me to continue building from the passion to help others sell well and feel good about this profession. I have learned from you, cheered you on, and celebrated your successes.

A special thank you to Michael Haubrich and Justus Morgan of Financial Service Group and Michael Goodman and the entire team at Wealthstream Advisors including Brenna McLoughlin, Brant Cavagnaro, Joe Orff, Katharine George, Matt Gordon, and Eric Siss. Also, I can't thank Brian Tegtmeyer, Joe Morgan, Ben and Deb Martinek, Rick Taborda, Jared Andreoli, John Munley, Charlie Horonzy, Chuck Goldblum, Joe Forish, Chaim Weinreb, Jenna VanLeeuwen, Luis Rosa, Damian Palfini, Ryan Lanagan, Sara Young, Rob Tilson, Eric Tilson, Anastasia Taber, Pam Horack, Brian Behl, Ed Coambs, and Sarah Kang, enough for continuing to show me the power of good financial advice. Your clients are lucky to have you in their corner and I am honored and deeply humbled to be welcomed into your life and business.

A big thank you to the guides, mentors, encouragers, and teachers who have surrounded me for decades. You keep me sharp, relevant, and knowing I am not alone in striving to help others sell well. That's you Colleen Stanley, Julie Hansen, Tonya Bjurstrom, Anita Nielsen, Lisa Magnuson, Lynn Hidy, Alice Heiman, Alice Kemper, Shawn Karol Sandy, Debbie Mrazek, Jill Konrath, Trish Bertuzzi, Lori Richardson, Bernadette McLelland, Andrea Waltz, Barbara Weaver Smith, Janice

Mars, Carole Mahoney, Caryn Kopp, Carol Moser, and Liz Heiman.

And those who also help advisors with all other aspects of building a thriving financial firm: Charesse Spiller, Zoe Meggert, Cameo Robertson, Brooklyn Brock, and Jen Goodman.

I also appreciate the financial industry leaders who inspire and encourage me to bring the best to the field: Alan Moore, Michael Kitces, Dr. Meghaan Lurtz, and Brendan Frazier.

In the decade since *Conversations That Sell* was published, it's been fun to watch my adult "kids," Kevin, Jackson, and Jenna Bleeke, move into their careers and continue to show me how communication is "done these days." Continue to move past any negativity about sales and you can go anywhere you want in life and career!

My dear "people" who are connected by genetics and by heart to encourage, support, and while often not knowing what I am talking about, still make me feel smart! Amy and Dan Kutz, Connie and JD Schreib, Lena Bredin, Beth Snyder, Jan Anthonsen, Chris Maruszewski, Michael Ragan, Rea Kaschak, and Mike Sanders.

Oh, and the birth family started by my long-deceased parents, who often weren't sure what "to do" about me but whose belief in me has kept me taking chances and seeking adventures. A shout out to my siblings who created the circumstances for me to want to be better at communication and stop family drama! Joe and Penny, Bill, Phil and Jeff, Shawn and Dana Noel and Collette and Jim Pleva.

And finally, I have deep appreciation for my team who worked through so many details and iterations of this book and all our training materials! Kevin Knight, who has the patience of a saint, Noreen Carballo, who jumped in for proofreading with a nanosecond notice, and Melissa Sandoval ensures great client experiences by being the keeper of all materials and shipping, your positive and energetic attitudes and belief in the work we do keeps us going. Thank you to Austin Delaney, Dana Kader Robb, Bernard Lustado, Kim Storz, Tracy Travis, Julie Points, and Nathan Knight who also support all our work—thank you!

PART I

Introduction

How It All Began

It was a dark, cold March evening during my senior year in college. While many other students were headed south to chase the sun, warm weather, and fun, I was headed to a job interview, where I would meet the branch manager of a small financial office in downtown Kenosha, Wisconsin … and I was nervous.

I wasn't yet sure what the "finance" job was or whether I was qualified. The office was small and dimly lit. The manager greeted me and handed me a clipboard with an assessment to complete before the interview and left me alone in the lobby.

Looking over the questions, I was concerned. "How many people do you know who have a retirement plan? Invest in the stock market? Own their own home?" I didn't know how to answer. Heck, I was a college student living on the cash I made from editing and typing other students' papers. I didn't really pay attention to real-life "adult" financial information.

Further questions on the questionnaire asked about my comfort with contacting friends and family with beneficial financial ideas. I answered truthfully, "Not comfortable at all."

I waited nervously as the manager reviewed my completed assessment, wondering if I should just leave. The whole "vibe" of the office and the assessment questions made me uncomfortable. It wasn't a welcoming environment, and the manager was very abrupt.

It seemed my responses to the questions weren't good for him either, as he came back to the lobby to tell me I failed his assessment and wasn't a good fit for what he was looking for. Of course, he was probably more professional than that, but the message that I should move on was clear.

I returned to my car, relieved. I don't know what responses failed me, but I was pretty sure it was about my lack of comfort in contacting my friends and family.

And that was when I thought I would *never* be in finance or in sales.

What a shame. Because now, with decades of working with finan-cial advisors in my rearview mirror, I know I could've been a good advisor! I know I could've passed the exams and provided excellent, professional, and knowledgeable service to people. I also know that the care I have for people would have made me trustworthy and that I would've helped so many people. But I wasn't comfortable contacting friends and family to "sell" something, so clearly was unsuited for these types of jobs.

Instead, I ended up in the financial industry as the head of train-ing and HR for a regional bank. I hired, trained, and often coached our tellers, investment bankers, mortgage loan officers, and commer-cial loan officers. I was in finance, but not in a direct client-facing role.

Even as I trained and coached bank employees, I still didn't love the sales aspect of finance. I still thought that most of the people on our team were more concerned with bonuses and incentives than with helping their clients.

It wasn't until I left the financial industry, pivoted to an HR posi-tion for a specialty toy company, and hired my own financial advisor to manage my stocks from the bank that I realized how wrong I was.

The toy business is where I "found" sales. As I hired a national sales team to accommodate a business model change and vetted sales training courses to unite our diverse sales team, I was flabbergasted to realize that I had been *in* sales my whole career! In HR, I was selling people job opportunities, policy and compliance, changes, and so much more. I learned that selling, when done with integrity, is the lifeblood of any company!

But what really led me to focus on serving advisors—and helping them build their business by developing their positive mindset, skills, and approach to selling—was having my own advisor!

I met Mike Haubrich, founder of Financial Service Group in Racine, Wisconsin, as we needed help with identifying how to best leverage my bank stocks.

Over time, Mike and I became friends and often exchanged business musings. In addition to my work at the toy company, I began to coach him, help him hire key team members (including 2 employees who have now been with the company for over 20 years), and provide training and process help. I consider my role at Financial Service Group one of my biggest professional successes: helping a team that was taking such good care of us, grow to serve more people!

When I mentioned that I was looking to leave corporate work and start a small business for flexibility when raising our three children, Mike encouraged me to offer my services to other advisors he knew. He thought my style, process-driven approach, and smarts were needed in the industry, and I should start a financial coaching business.

I'm glad I took his advice. 20+ years later, I am fully ensconced in the financial industry, driven by a passion for helping advisors get out of their own way so they can sell well without losing their soul, and thus help so many more people! I love my work and clients, and I often joke (and lament) that I would have had a higher income and worked fewer hours if I would've just become an advisor 20 years ago.

And here I am now with a powerful message about ethical selling practices and an approach that allows you to start giving value to your prospects from that first interaction!

I'm humbled to realize that thousands of advisors have adopted the process outlined in this book. I'm honored to have worked with these advisors to build the business, and career, they deserve. And I am in awe of the dedication and heart that advisors bring to their work.

The strategies and tools in these pages will allow you to do the same.

CHAPTER 1

The Importance of YOU in Selling Financial Services

"Always be a first-rate version of yourself,
instead of a second-rate version of somebody else."

—Judy Garland

With today's constant bombardment of online marketing messages and the push to conduct most financial transactions online, it can seem that the personalization of financial business is gone. It may seem that you, the human advisor, are facing a challenging battle in your quest to help people with their finances.

And now with AI everywhere, even the seasoned advisors I know are concerned that the bots will replace advisors. What a shame! Though financial information is pervasive, it is also overwhelming to sift through, and so many people won't put in the time and mental effort to do so, which means *you* are more important than ever.

What? The advisor is more important than ever?

Yes, you read that correctly. *You* are an essential component of what you offer. *You* are essential to the confidence and conviction of your prospects' decision-making.

The Bots Will Not Replace You

What's the last "robo" or AI product that created fear and shouts of "we're going to be replaced" by technology? It seems almost every week a new fintech or outbound marketing tool can replace you. For decades now, "experts" have been raising concerns about the demise of humans in advising. Yet I haven't seen that happen, and I don't expect it will.

First, it's been found that more than half of Americans are unaware of robo-advisors.[1] And while many do find help through online financial solutions, these solutions cannot do everything a human advisor can do. Technology currently can't provide the emotional support and human connection that people need but often miss when they decide to *do* something about their finances: staying on the course of implementation, feeling good about how they are doing, using a thought partner to make confident decisions.

While AI has a place in the financial industry for efficient routine activities, it won't replace the human element for many aspects of financial advice in the near future.

This confirms my conviction that human advisors will always be needed to help people in a "live" way—whether face-to-face or virtually.

Why is that? Because finances are personal. People's stories are personal. And because deciding to get financial help isn't easy!

Bringing You to the Forefront

Additionally, many people, no matter their education level, don't know how to "buy" what you offer. They may have never sought out financial services before. Or they may have only had poor experiences

---

[1] Kineree Shah, "Americans More Likely to Trust a Robo-Adviser than Human Financial Advice," YouGov, March 29, 2023, https://business.yougov.com/content/46416-americans-more-likely-to-trust-a-robo-adviser-than-human-financial-advice.

in the past—whether personal or through advertising or entertainment media—with product-pushing "advisors."

So, prospects may "show up" in product-buying mode, focused on data and facts (ahem, fees!). Or they may be unsure of what to focus on. And you, the advisor, can guide them to focus on what does matter: having support and expertise.

Or maybe the prospective client has researched what they should do or talked with others, and they are smack in the middle of the process of sorting through the plethora of information available. It's enough to make the smartest and savviest of prospects get brain drain!

That's why *you* are often the differentiating factor in a prospect's confidence to work with someone. While fees, the process, and the service itself are important, what makes a prospect choose your firm over your competitor's is often YOU—your understanding of their situation, your concern for their needs, your ideas about how they might best get started, and the confidence you give them in your knowledge. In short, they need what *you* personally bring to the sales process and solution before, during, and after the decision to work with you is made.

Let me share an example from my own experience.

Early in my sales career, a mentor told me I would win more business if I focused more on my product during sales conversations. I was selling training materials and workshops, not selling my personal expertise … or so I thought. I had modeled myself—style, dress, and demeanor—after a certain successful sales professional in my industry to compensate for my young age. And, my mentor's message was that I shouldn't worry about my experience (or lack thereof), as the product would sell itself if I didn't get in the way.

And I believed her because, after all, I was the youngest consultant in the group. Why would anyone think I could personally help their financial advisors become stronger in sales, communication, and service?

As a young upstart business owner, my confidence was low, and I thought she knew it all. She said I should not "call attention" to myself and just keep everyone focused on the product. Well, that was okay by me. In fact, it felt like less pressure!

But that well-meaning, old-school coaching nearly cost me my first big sales opportunity—a multiyear training engagement in the financial services industry.

While I managed to land the project after some quick scrambling, the impact was costly: tens of thousands of dollars over a 4-year period and a bruised ego. Why? Because I focused on the product and didn't support its delivery that included my experience and abilities. I lost sight of the value I added to the solution and, of course then, so did the client. Bottom line, they wanted the *product*, but they didn't want me.

Nope, they did not want me working with their advisors. They wanted someone who they knew their advisors could relate to and connect with. And this next part will make some of you wince, but it is what happened. They wanted me to "bring them" an older male, preferably bald, and it was a bonus if he had military experience. Seriously, I am not making this up!

I salvaged the opportunity and found a trainer who matched their profile perfectly to deliver the workshops. Unfortunately, the percentage I paid him cut deep into my profits, and over the years, I lost many important referrals that went to him as the front man.

Gradually, as I served as the account manager and liaison in support of the training workshops my front "man" delivered for this client, I gained confidence and began demonstrating my competence as a resource for the client. I had plenty of opportunities to solve problems (even ones I wasn't responsible for), drive ongoing implementation, offer my experience and advice, and use my project management and organization talents to "get it done."

After one particularly productive meeting where I shared some of my knowledge, insight, and suggestions, one of the leaders who had been on the original selection team asked, "Where were *you* during the sales process?"

I wanted to stammer, "What? Where was I? I was the one working 12-hour days to meet your deadlines and compile the information requested by your 13-person decision team each and every step of the way." Wisely, I kept my mouth shut as she went on to say that if the decision team had seen how smart, knowledgeable, funny, and personable I was, I wouldn't have needed to bring in my training colleague!

Hearing that hard truth was tough, but it taught me the importance of being *me* during the sales process—of letting my personality and unique strengths come through. If only I hadn't hidden behind the product, thinking that was all that mattered. If only I hadn't blindly followed my mentor's direction to focus only on the product and not incorporate "me" into the process and solution. If only I had demonstrated that I was part of the solution and the value they would receive, I would have had some fantastic experiences working with their teams, with fewer complications and a much higher profit.

Instead, I showed up as an imposter—acting like my mentor, not me.

Imposter Syndrome, Anyone?

Have you experienced imposter syndrome? It's real and we embody it when we focus prospective clients solely on the process, service, or solution. Maybe you have had this feeling of not being "worthy" in showcasing your role in the solution.

Maybe you don't want to be seen as assertive or pushy. After all who wants to be "that person"? Or maybe you're feeling the pressure of needing income, meeting an expectation, or reaching your goals to help more clients because that's what drives you. Or maybe you are convinced that your age, gender, experience level, lifestyle, or other personal factors will be a barrier. Maybe you are new to the whole business of sales and feel uncomfortable and unskilled. The reasons for the imposter feeling are many!

You may have well-meaning mentors, colleagues, and managers

advise you to "fake it 'til you make it" when you're fighting through the fear, stress, and uncertainty in selling situations. But this certainly doesn't work well in many situations, does it? Prospective clients have too many pressures on their time, resources, and attention to waste on advisors who are disingenuous. And trust me, people can spot a fake a mile away, which leads to a lack of building trust and confidence. Prospects need advisors who really care, who really understand, who really can help them focus on the important information and discard all the rest. They need advisors who show up prepared to work with, and sometimes guide them through, the information *they* need to process to make that first important decision: to work with *you*!

But what if you genuinely lack confidence, or perhaps the necessary skills or experience, to be the kind of advisor you think prospects need today? That might be why you're reading this book. Be assured, you've come to the right place. The rest of this book will introduce you to sales strategies, skills, tools, best practices, and examples that will help you approach any selling situation with genuine confidence that you are a competent, valuable resource for your prospects.

And you will need that—confidence and a solid reputation, both in person and online. In today's transparent world, your reputation, and that of your firm or company, is exposed 24/7.

For you as an advisor, this transparency is a double-edged sword. It opens opportunities to reach more prospects, build stronger relationships and trust, and differentiate yourself from the competition. At the same time, it also leaves all you have ever done uncovered for your prospects and competition to view and analyze.

When prospective clients access the internet or their real-life network for information about you, they easily find others' experiences. One bad experience or questionable action can be broadcast instantly across the internet or through social media and consumer forum sites. And, oh boy, do people pay attention. There's simply nowhere to hide and no room for faking it these days.

So, I am glad you're reading this book. Stick with me in the coming chapters, and the transparency of the world and the fact that others can spot a fake will be a benefit, not a hindrance, for you.

Adopt and Adapt Best Practices to Escalate Your Value and Sales

One of the many things I love about this industry is the sharing of best practices online, at conferences, in study groups, and in open hours. You've learned you don't have to "reinvent the wheel" as they say.

BUT ... (yes, it's a big BUT!)

Best practices aren't universally the best. What works for one specific advisor or firm may not fully transfer to you and your firm. The key is to adopt and *adapt* best practices—to make them your own.

I know that what you'll find in these pages works—best practices for sales conversations. Thousands of advisor successes allow me to be that confident.

I also know you can lead a "textbook sales conversation" and it won't work 100% of the time. People and situations are unique. You can't control the biggest variable—your prospect!

The reasonable takeaway from the valuable content in this book is to *increase* your probability of success. To increase your conversion rate by being genuine.

Take the frameworks, best practices, and suggested language in this book and try them on for size. Practice them and make incremental adjustments to best fit your service model, your style, the situations you encounter, and most importantly your prospects. Make them genuinely yours by adapting them to fit your strengths, personality, skills, and expertise.

When you don't settle for faking it and applying the best practices in a rote way that a bot could do and are genuinely "you," a vital part of your solution, you give your prospects confidence. This leads you both to confidently take the first steps in working together.

CHAPTER 2

Collaborative Selling: Where Every Conversation Counts and Everyone Wins

Collaborative selling is a human-first approach that allows everything to be easier for the prospect, and thus you.

—A Nancy Timely Tip

Many of the prospects who you talk with have no idea how to "buy" what you offer, as mentioned in the last chapter. Complicating this further, many people don't seek financial support and help in the first place. Even though 62% of Americans say they need to improve their financial situation, only 35% seek the help of a professional financial advisor, according to a survey of 2,381 US adults released by Northwestern Mutual[2].

How many don't seek help because of the negative connotations surrounding financial service sales? Those who do seek help may have

---

[2]   Vance Cariaga, "Survey: Most Americans Don't Use Financial Advisors — How is That Changing Because of COVID, Inflation and Economic Uncertainty?" Yahoo!Finance, August 1, 2022, https://finance.yahoo.com/news/survey-most-americans-don-t-163904564.html

had past experiences in sales situations where they felt "sold to," or they may treat this "purchase" like they are buying a TV or laptop! And if prospects approach the conversation with you as if they are on the opposite side of the table, it makes everything harder.

Imagine this scenario. You're in a conversation, directly across from your prospect—maybe one person, a couple, a family, or even a business team—with space between you. The space has clutter, maybe it's computer screens, documents, a laptop, tablet, mobile phones, or cups or mugs. Your prospective client is possibly fidgety and avoids direct eye contact, afraid that you'll try to *sell* them something or *tell* them something they must do.

Now imagine a different scenario. You enter the office, conference room, living room, or virtual video room and the prospect smiles at you and greets you. If you're lucky enough for an in-person situation, you may also receive a warm handshake or a hug! The prospect is open when responding to your questions and engages with you collaboratively to discuss how you and your service might help them or provide something they want or need.

In which scenario do you have a better chance of succeeding? The second one, of course!

How do you make that happen? How do you create such a setting? By approaching each sales conversation using the collaborative selling approach you'll learn in this book.

Collaborative Selling: What It Is and Why It Works

Collaborative selling is a human-first approach that allows everything to be easier for the prospect, and thus you.

Collaborative selling is working with your prospect to help them *do* or *decide* something.

It's a conversation, an information exchange, that YOU lead to guide them through their decision-making process. It's about being on the same side, working side by side *with* your prospect to achieve something you both want. They want a solution, and you want to help and serve them. That's what you saw in the second scenario.

Focusing on the prospect and on collaboration—collaborative selling—is how you achieve what you both want. When your focus is on helping your prospect solve a problem, capture an opportunity, or get what they want or need, you give them greater value, build a trusting relationship, and earn their loyalty and referrals. That's how you create a situation where you both achieve what you want or need—short term and long term.

To help you remember the importance of focusing on your prospect throughout the selling process, I've developed an acronym—WiifT, pronounced "whiff-it"—which stands for "**What's in it for Them?**" The Them is your prospect. The *T* is capitalized to emphasize that the focus is on *Them*.

A WiifT focus makes the decision-making process easy, and easy is better for everyone involved.

How do you become and remain WiifT focused? That's what the remainder of this book will outline for you.

As an overview, a WiifT approach in your conversations, and in your overall selling process, focuses on the prospects' Problems, Opportunities, Wants, and Needs, which forms another important acronym: POWNs, pronounced with the sound of the o in *town*. In collaborative selling, the prospect's problems, opportunities, wants, and needs are the areas you work to address or achieve. (I promise there are only five acronyms in this book for you to remember.)

Often, advisors are taught to find the prospect's need or pain. And while that is a place to start, when you look beyond the obvious want or need and help your prospect capture *opportunities* and solve *problems*, you gain their respect, earn their trust, give greater value, and create a stronger sense of urgency for adopting your solution.

When you explore the context and situation beyond immediate wants and needs, make it human first, and bring emotions, as appropriate, into the conversation, you make a huge difference to your prospect. You will be immediately more valuable than someone who is only focused on a product or service transaction.

While we know collaboration is effective, some misunderstand what collaboration is. There is a perception that collaboration is an arduous process, involving large teams of people and long timelines. Yet collaborative selling can be as simple as a single conversation or a string of conversations between a prospect and an advisor—two-way conversations where the discoveries and information exchanged are part of the value the prospect receives.

In a nutshell, collaborative selling involves a prospect and advisor working together, conversation by conversation, to address the prospect's POWNs, with the outcome being that they both achieve something of value. This approach works whether your conversations take place face-to-face, by video, over the phone, or through email.

Collaboration Is Consultation Plus

Consultative selling has been the term used for many years, and it positions you, the advisor, as the expert in your field—the authority on your product or service. Your role has been to uncover your prospect's wants and needs, develop a solution you recommend, and then return to explain how your solution matches that prospect's need. But this is a "them and us" mindset, not a "working together" approach.

Although the consultative approach has been extremely effective for decades, it typically only addresses the prospect's wants and needs while missing opportunities and problems. Collaborative selling provides an opportunity to add much more value, as I'll explain later in this discussion.

Collaborative selling is also a more efficient sales process because it addresses the fact that prospects face more challenges in their life than ever before. I call this the "More and Less" syndrome.

Today's prospects face:

More	Less
Information	Expectations
Stress	Confidence
Time	Patience

That's why prospects welcome an efficient and effective selling approach that doesn't waste their time or energy or adds to their "More and Less" challenges. You need to make every conversation count for your prospect, and that's what happens when you focus on WiifT because your prospect becomes a part of the solution.

Remember the old saying, "Two heads are better than one?" When you and the prospect bring your collective expertise and ideas together, you often come up with a solution that neither of you would have discovered alone.

What collaboration looks like: An advisor in one of my training cohorts shared that one of his prospects objected to the amount of time and work it would take to create the financial plan. Rather than quickly suggesting a solution to the concern, the advisor asked the prospect for their suggestion on how to make it more efficient for them. The prospect's suggested solution was one the advisor never would have thought of, leading the prospect to feel part of the solution and quickly commit to working together.

When you collaborate, your conversations become relevant for both you and the prospect, and you reduce the prospect's fear or irritation of being "sold to" or "told to." Better ideas are cultivated and earlier buy-in is achieved, making the final sales decision much easier to secure. Prospect conversions and goals are achieved more efficiently, which is exactly what today's "More and Less" prospect needs.

CHAPTER 3

When You Collaborate, Everyone Wins

When all parties work together,
all stakeholders win. It's a win-win-win or Win³™.

—A Nancy Timely Tip

Collaborative selling focuses on working with the prospect to address their POWNs. But make no mistake, this does *not* mean that you, the advisor, and your firm are unimportant. No, the winning solution or outcome benefits everyone involved.

In a traditional win-win situation, the goal is for two stakeholders—typically the prospect and the company—to win. With collaborative selling, you personally are also an important stakeholder.

When all parties work together, all stakeholders win. It's a win-win-win or Win³™ (I call this "win-cubed").

For you solo RIAs and advisors out there, Win³ is very important to you. Treating your business and yourself as separate entities who must both win when a new client relationship begins is important. It keeps you from discounting too much, ensures your scope of services is honored, and takes some of the pressure off you!

Graphic 3-1 represents the Win³ model, illustrating the interconnectivity of the stakeholders. The center components of the model are the how-tos for accomplishing the triple win, the Win^3.

Graphic 3-1

What Win^3 Looks Like

What does a Win^3 win look like? How do each of these stakeholders win? Well, when the prospect decides to work with you and their POWNs are successfully addressed, it creates a large Winner's Circle that *you* made.

Your client wins by having a solution to their POWNs. They may benefit in any number of ways: more time for hobbies, less stress, more money or savings, better family relationships, peace of mind, captured opportunities, enhanced reputations, resolved problems, and fulfilled needs or wants. They also gain a trusted advisor and thought partner on their side.

Your company wins with increased revenue, community or industry acknowledgment, loyal client retention, increased organic referrals, higher profit margins, higher team retention, and a good reputation.

You, the advisor, win personal satisfaction from using your knowledge, more income, improved lifestyle, less nagging from your spouse, children who adore you, and a parade in your honor (oh, that's a bit much isn't it?).

What makes collaborative selling unique is that stronger prospect relationships and value are provided from the very first interaction, which quickly leads to loyalty and referrals. You also become a valuable part of the solution, as we discussed in Chapter 1, and that builds greater confidence, which leads to more of everything. Now we're talking Win^3!

What's more, the ripple effect of winning extends beyond the Win^3. Additional stakeholders also win. These include the client's family and friends, your company's shareholders, and associates within your company who support you and service the client. And let's add to your personal benefits with stakeholders, including family and friends, because your well-being and financial success affect them too. When a collaborative sale is made, and the prospect's POWNs are addressed, wins happen all around!

About now you may be wondering, "Is it really possible for all the stakeholders to win?" It is possible when you focus on the components in the middle of the Win^3 model.

Conversation by Conversation, What Collaboration Looks Like

While collaborative selling might sound good in theory, it may be hard for you to picture how it really works. Let me illustrate with an example from my own experience.

I met advisor Ed Coambs at a conference. We engaged in conversation about his business and what he wanted to create with it. We also discussed personal questions and observations about life.

I suggested that we have a one-on-one conversation the next week, where we could better focus on helping him determine initial actions he could take to convert more of his prospects. Then, if he wanted to discuss how my services could support his now-defined priorities, we would schedule another conversation.

Over the course of two Zoom conversations, we got to know each other personally. I learned that Ed had a big, brilliant vision of building a Therapy-Informed Financial Planning™ team of over 100 advisors who would integrate financial planning and therapy concepts into their service offering.

He was less than a year into his RIA but wasn't sure where to focus first. In our first meeting, we discussed his options and reviewed pros and cons. I then sent him a follow-up email highlighting what we discussed and outlining questions to help him determine his priorities. We met again, and he decided to address his sales situation first.

Ed wanted to increase his conversion rate significantly and have a process for re-engaging the 60 stalled prospects he had collected. He realized that building a process he could follow would make him more efficient and that this process could also be followed by advisors on his team.

His low conversion rate had left people without the help they needed. It also left Ed's firm, Healthy Love and Money, without the revenue needed to scale, and left Ed personally seeking more income. (Notice how he was unknowingly looking for a Win^3?)

Ed said he didn't feel like he was in a "sale" during our time together, that we were just having a conversation. It gave him the hope and conviction that he could set that dynamic up with his prospects too.

While not every selling situation requires the same level of collaboration, it was powerful in this case and for this type of decision-maker. If I had followed the typical path of telling him what he had to do, I might not have earned his trust. I can't wait to continue to watch what he will do in these next years.

Here's an advisor example: Kurt, a financial advisor, met with a couple discussing their lifestyle dreams, their plan for funding their children's education and weddings, and the vacation they wanted to take for their 25th anniversary.

Kurt asked questions of both the husband and wife for clarity and facilitated the dialogue between them to ensure their priorities were in sync. He then provided an overview of how he would help them achieve these financial goals. Kurt asked for their thoughts and feelings about various options, referencing their existing financial investments and budget and their need for insurance. He helped them synchronize their goals, their concerns, and their overall approach to how they worked together.

At the end of the conversation, Kurt committed to creating an initial recommendation plan to outline how they would work together to achieve what they had discussed. They agreed on the date and time they would reconvene to review the recommendation.

During their next conversation, Kurt recapped their first discussion, asked what there was to clarify or add, and then shared his initial ideas while connecting them back to their goals (the WiifTs) and their earlier discussion. He asked for their input, comments, and questions, and then asked if they were ready to officially start the process. They were.

That's a collaboration! They worked through the process together, and the decision to work together benefitted the couple as well as Kurt and his firm.

The Inside of Win³

Now you have a vision of what winning looks like. But how do you accomplish this? By embodying the three terms in the middle of the Win³ model: Genuine, WiifT-focused, and Collaborative. These are the What to Dos for collaborative selling! Most of this book will outline the how-tos that allow you to be genuine, focused on Them, and collaborative along the way.

CHAPTER 4

Collaborative Selling in Challenging Situations

I can't deny that there are some predicable
situations where collaborative selling
can be a particular challenge.

—A Nancy Timely Tip

At this point you may be thinking, "Those are great examples, except what about this situation—or that? What about the scenarios I find myself in? Does the collaborative selling approach always work?"

I'd like to respond with an absolute yes, but that would be a lie. As I mentioned earlier, there are no absolutes in anything that involves people!

I can't deny that in some predicable situations, collaborative selling can be challenging. You may encounter some of these more common ones noted in the following pages.

The Order-Dictating Prospect Challenge

While your intentions and approach may not be rooted in "old school" selling, some prospects haven't made the switch yet. Some are conditioned to expect you to simply take their "order" or provide a solution. They either tell you what they want and expect you to find a way to get it to them, or they say, "Tell me what you will do for me—oh, and make it cheap, fast, and have a guaranteed 12% annual return!"

This is a challenge and it can be tough, but not impossible, for prospects to switch from being an order-dictator to a collaborator. In these situations, adjust your approach and conversation to guide the prospect, including them in each step whenever possible.

That's what I did in the following situation. I once worked with a firm founder who told me he knew exactly how to equip his team to start boosting sales within his firm. He had done his research and had years of his own experience in selling to prospects—that's how he built his 12-person team! At first, he seemed like a dream come true. He came to me to fill a specific need. He had prequalified himself, done his research on me and my services, and just wanted a fee quote. In essence, he wanted to "place an order."

Yet, in talking with him to get the specifics needed to develop the scope of service, I realized that what he was asking for would not get him what he wanted. It would fail. And that would prevent him from reaching his goal, which was to decrease his company's dependence on him being the "rainmaker."

I asked him if he was willing to consider additional information and options, and he was hesitant. He said he knew his team and all they needed was "some training." He was adamant he didn't need a "consultant"; all he wanted was a fee quote to "come in and run some workshops." I then explained that I might not be the right solution for him after all. I would not waste his time or money on implementing something that would not get him where he wanted to go. And, yes, I was willing to walk away if necessary. I knew I wouldn't have been successful in the long term following his lead, and the agony along the way was not worth my time and energy.

After I explained this, he paused and agreed to give me an hour to discuss his situation further. What we discovered, together, was that we could build the right implementation plan for his team. This "rightsizing" would provide him with the outcome he needed and allow my team to make an impact on his advisors in a shorter time frame. After involving a few key advisors for buy-in, the decision to work together was made the next week.

While this interaction led to a conversion, many did not. Walking away wasn't always easy. One man even told me he was sure I did not know what I was doing, and he was glad we wouldn't work together. Fortunately, I was too! Not working together was the best decision for everyone involved.

What does all this mean? If the order they want to place is best for them, run with it. If it is not best for them, tell them! And try to further engage them in a collaborative sales conversation. If they don't want it, it's okay to walk away.

The Misfit Prospect Challenge

When a prospect has ideas that aren't in alignment with what you do and how you work—whether in terms of your approach, their investment philosophy, their fee tolerance, their timing, their expectations, their processes, or their unwillingness to disclose necessary information or take advice—collaboration is going to be tough. I've had prospects who wanted me to help their sales teams learn how to coerce prospects into action with hard closes, even when their prospects weren't ready. Others asked me to help their advisors pitch a solution without regard to whether their prospect was qualified or interested. Neither type of request was in sync with my philosophy and approach to selling. These were misfits for my services and me personally.

When it's obvious that a potential prospect is not a fit, I've learned—the hard way, I assure you—that I will be more productive, happier, and have less stress if I move on to higher-probability prospects as early as possible.

And this is where I have seen brilliance from many advisors in prequalifying prospects. While that is not the focus of this book, read the many online financial advisor forums and you'll see the stories—some are quite entertaining.

For me, if someone isn't willing to discuss their openness to change and to pay for service, they are taking away precious time from my current clients and my business. And the sooner we part, the better.

If you think you're not in a position to walk away, look at what the most successful people do: they focus their time and energy on high-probability prospects. As one top advisor told me, "When I learned the value of using the delete key, my business grew."

The E-Relationship Challenge

Another complication in selling collaboratively is the prospect who wants or expects the "e-relationship." They prefer a "send me this" or "click on this link" approach to communication and the selling process and service. This can work if you have set up your sales process and service model to deliver that way. But more collaborative advisors want the human connection and relationship.

While we should take advantage of electronic tools and technology to enhance the sales process, an e-relationship presents unique challenges when it's our main, or only, mode of communication. Instead of a two-way conversation with both parties engaged, we may end up with two streams of one-way communications and less opportunity to discover POWNs and motivations. This makes it more challenging to differentiate our solutions from the competition's.

I've worked with several prospects—and have existing clients—who prefer to handle most of our conversations through email. And I respect that ... to a point.

When we start to revisit the same questions and virtually send the same information back and forth, I rely on my three-back-and-forth guideline—that if we go back and forth three times on the same topic, I call or send an email saying, "Now that we've gone back and forth a few times with email, let's expedite the rest with a 15-minute phone call. What times work for you?" What's surprising is that often the answer is, "Call me now. I'm available."

If the prospect prefers to maintain an e-relationship, adapt your communication to include extra documentation and follow-up. Keep your messages short and include questions, specific examples, and relevant attachments.

Time Pressure Challenges

Initial collaborative conversations can sometimes take a little longer than a "show up and throw up" sales call, and you may need to spend more time preparing to ensure that each conversation is productive and focused on WiifT.

Some advisors feel the initial sales conversation should take 10 to 15 minutes. And if you're in a busy environment, it may seem impossible to take more time for a collaborative approach. While I am not advocating that the first conversation must be *any* certain length, I've found that it's more important to identify what must happen in the conversation and determine the amount of time it takes to accomplish that objective.

It's why AJ Ayers, co-founder of Brooklyn Fi, and her team took a hard look at their 15-minute Discovery Call. Because they know their ideal client behaviors so well, they created the most efficient process I've ever seen. By requiring prospective clients to watch pre-meeting educational videos and complete a "Quick Fit Quiz," her team uses their Discovery Calls to connect clients to the right service more quickly. In working together to uplevel their process, we identified that in addition to a few other process adjustments, adding just 5 more minutes to their Discovery Call would allow them more time to establish the next step: signing the Agreement. After 4 months, AJ reported, "15 minutes was perhaps too short and rushed for the prospect, and adding 5 minutes allows us more flexibility."

While Brooklyn Fi has found success with 20-minute Discovery Calls, other advisors find success with 90-minute Discovery Calls. What matters is having a systematic approach to the conversation with a specific objective. You'll determine what works based on your process, niche, and objective for each conversation.

I can assure you that many advisors have adapted the systematic conversation framework we will cover in Chapter 5 to make their conversations efficient and value focused. And if it does take a little longer on the first call, it's time well spent, because the information exchange early in the conversation shortens the overall selling process and saves time in the long run.

Is Collaborative Selling Worth the Effort?

Potential challenges occur with any approach to selling, and collaborative selling is no different. But as you read through the tips and strategies outlined in the upcoming chapters, I'm confident you'll decide that it's in your best interest to adopt and adapt these collaborative and WiifT-focused strategies. And, as a client recently reminded me, the strategies are also in the best interest of the prospect.

These strategies may seem like extra work at first, and I won't say that collaborative selling is *easier*. What I have found, though, is that it's a matter of transferring energies and actions rather than adding more. It's a matter of getting comfortable with the new strategies— and adapting them to make them your own.

If you elected to read this book, you most likely believe that relationships are important—relationships that lead to repeat business, referrals, and loyal clients—and if so, you will find that the effort of collaborating is well worth it.

CHAPTER 5

Systematized Success: Make Every Conversation Count

"At its core, a fully functioning business is basically a set of systems and processes."

—John Jantsch, renowned small business marketing guru

The Merriam-Webster Dictionary defines a system as an "organized or established procedure, arrangement, or pattern."[3] We know this to be true: the financial industry runs on systems … many systems! Marketing systems, technology systems, and oh, so many operating systems that make for a successful firm!

Advisors typically LOVE systems, processes, and workflows, too. And why? Simply put, systems work! A system helps us get stuff done.

Better yet, a good system helps us get stuff done with less effort and less time, as well as more consistency, repeatability, reliability, and confidence. We create good systems by examining, evaluating, and adjusting the patterns of our successes. When we do this with productive, collaborative sales conversations, we create a roadmap that increases confidence, efficiency, and positive outcomes.

---

[3] Merriam-Webster online, s.v., "system," accessed April 2024, https://www.merriam-webster.com/dictionary/system.

Five Steps to Systematic Sales Success

Think about your last successful conversation. How did you succeed with your last prospect? How did you guide them through their decision-making process to confidently say yes? Can you specifically identify every action and step, the flow of your conversation, and what worked well? With a lot of thought, you probably can track *how* you did *what* you did—from opening the conversation to closing and getting the yes decision.

This is because you are already, consciously or unconsciously, using a system for your sales conversations. You have already established a routine and a way of leading the conversation. Even if it isn't working well, or you use it inconsistently, you have a flow to the conversations you lead.

Your routine may have been adopted over the years or as a crash-and-burn effort where you did what you thought you should at the time, and it didn't bode well for you or the prospects. If you've been selling for years, your system has likely become very comfortable for you. You may even work through your sales conversations without a lot of thought about how you're doing it.

Whatever routine you have now produces your current level of success. If you are satisfied with your results currently, then you probably don't need the ideas and tools in this book.

But if you are like the advisors I know, you may wonder, "How do I convert more?" "How can I capture more clients, in less time, and with more ease?" and "How do I help prospects see the value I offer?"

Successful advisors look for incremental adjustments in their selling to help them and their firms. This attitude of continual improvement is why I really enjoy working with advisors. They often discover that going back to the basics for their sales conversations can easily catapult their sales by 5 or 10% or even higher. Jonathan Grannick, a San Diego–based advisor, adopted the collaborative conversation system and increased his conversion rate from 26% to 60%.

New advisors benefit from this approach as well. If you are new to this sales thing and want to shortcut the trial-and-error process to quickly ramp up your client base, this system will meet your need for speed.

Fortunately, you don't have to go to all the trouble of constructing a system that will lead to more sales conversation success. The 5-Step Sales System I'm about to outline—WIIFT®—was developed by observing thousands of advisor conversations over the last decades. And it is continually sharpened through feedback from advisors during my workshop, watching recorded advisor conversations, and coaching time.

This system may challenge your current practices and actions. It may challenge long-held beliefs about selling. I ask that you put your assumptions, ego, and current beliefs on hold and objectively consider adjustments to your approach that may elevate your sales in a short time.

The WIIFT® Sales System guides you toward a greater probability of success in every conversation, allowing you to:

- Ensure success with consistent and conscious actions
- Replicate it over and over in all situations, with minor adjustments
- Diagnose gaps in stalled sales or troublesome situations, allowing you to reengage and possibly help them get to a yes

Graphic 5-1

WIIFT

I've purposely used the same letters as the acronym from Chapter 2 for this system. I've done this to give double meaning to the phrase What's in it for Them (WiifT). Here, WIIFT, in all caps, is the 5-Step System that will guide you and keep you focused on What's in it for Them to make every conversation count.

Graphic 5–1, shown on the previous page, is your visual aid to the system that allows you to capture that Win^3 described in Chapter 3. You'll notice that each component of the graphic represents a key principle to collaborative selling success:

Prove is the umbrella over the whole system, present throughout the sales conversation and any interaction you have. It begins before the conversation and is present in every action you take or don't take for the entire sales process and relationship.

Prepare is the foundation of your conversation. Preparation makes every aspect of your conversation more effective.

The 5 steps of the system—**W**ait, **I**nitiate, **I**nvestigate, **F**acilitate, and **T**hen Consolidate (WIIFT)—are in the middle of the model as the center of your conversation success.

Did you notice that the conversation happens between the two red dots? The dots represent you! They indicate your involvement from beginning to end of the conversation. Your genuine expertise, credibility, and experiences are critical components in this equation. You are the guide and leader of the entire system!

You'll be further introduced to the components of this system in the next chapter.

CHAPTER 6

The Steps for Collaborative Sales Conversations

Robotic use of the WIIFT system is not the goal.
It is not so specific and prescriptive that it
removes individuality. To keep yourself genuine,
adjust the steps and tools to best fit your style,
company processes, and client types.

—A Nancy Timely Tip

We begin our overview of the WIIFT model at the center, with a brief
introduction to each of the 5 steps that form the WIIFT acronym.
Then focus on the "cocoon" of Prove and Prepare. In later chapters,
we'll dive deeper into each step, exploring each step's objectives, how-
tos, and examples.

Step 1: Wait

Just as the first step of every system launches what is to come, the *Wait* step forms the foundation of your collaborative conversation success, as it allows you to maximize the value of the time with your prospect as you prepare for the specific conversation. This step focuses on you making time for proper preparation in advance of the conversation. We'll talk more about preparation in the next chapter.

The *Wait* step's benefits are often missed for two main reasons: time constraints and overconfidence. Each of these is nonsense, quite frankly, because as I'll comment on later, it does not take extra time to prepare, and overconfidence often leads to overtalking and making assumptions that may trip up the opportunity. The good news is that productive preparation is within your reach!

As you look at the WIIFT graphic, you'll notice the *W* is different from the rest of the letters. That's to denote that the *Wait* step is the only step completely in your control. You either do the prep, or you don't. Your prospect is not involved.

When you are prepped, you're ready to lead the conversation with the next step.

Step 2: Initiate

Initiate sets the stage for what is to come. The critical objective of Initiate is to "earn the right" to an open information exchange in the rest of the conversation.

Initiate officially begins the conversation, and your connection, with the prospect. It is applicable to the opening moments of every conversation (including client meetings). It includes your greeting and introduction, confirms the reason for, as well as the time allotted, for the conversation, allows you to connect with the person before turning to the agreed-upon agenda, and begins the collaboration. Even if you know the person or people, a good initiation makes a productive start to each conversation.

An effective *Initiation* opens the door to a value-filled conversation and connects you with the prospect to build trust, engage them, and specifically earn the right to ask questions they will fully answer.

Yes, the *right to ask*. Permission to talk about their situation and the factors around it is earned by demonstrating your focus on "What's in it for Them?" from the very start.

Step 3: Investigate

From *Initiate*, your conversation easily flows into *Investigate*. This is the discovery part of the conversation! I'm sure you *know* you are supposed to ask questions—the key is to ask *relevant, open-ended* questions that get the prospect talking about their story and its impact while you actively listen, take notes, paraphrase, and ask follow-up questions.

The *Investigate* step in WIIFT guides you to identify their story with the facts and emotions around their problems, opportunities, wants, and needs (the POWNs introduced in Chapter 2). It also qualifies the prospect and clarifies the sense of urgency and commitment to addressing their POWNs.

Investigating is more than fact-finding for needs and "pain points." Although that is important, you'll expand your understanding of what the prospect values and the potential for collaboration by discovering and exploring the prospect's POWNs. When you also explore the Risks and Rewards or impact of their current situation and future potential outcomes, you'll uncover the value needed to convert the prospect.

As you *Investigate*, the broad, strategic questions allow the opportunity to go beyond just looking for their pain and needs by:

🖔 Exploring, reviewing, and addressing the prospect's current needs, wants, or problems, as well as their concerns for the future

🖔 Aiding the person in capturing opportunities for their situation that they might not have considered

🖔 Exploring the emotional aspects of the situation

Why is it important to explore the emotional aspects of the prospect and situation? Even though most prospects make their case or decision with logic, emotions are often the true underlying motivator to the decision.

The information gathered and discovered together during *Investigation*, including whether this is a qualified prospect of your solution, opens additional potential for collaborating in the next step.

When you know their story, you have earned the right to facilitate the specifics of your solution.

Step 4: Facilitate

While the *Investigate* step is the crux for most consultative sales systems, collaborative conversations require at least as much emphasis on the *Facilitate* step.

Why *Facilitate*? Because according to Merriam-Webster.com, the definition of *Facilitate* is "to make (something) easy or easier."

This is exactly what we need to do: make it easy for the prospect to "get it" and to understand the value and outcomes of working together. We do this by demonstrating the value of our solution in how it addresses their specific POWNs and impacts Them.

The key skills for *Facilitating* collaborative sales conversations lead us to "rightsizing" all the information as you educate, recommend, and collaboratively explore how your solutions provide value to *that* prospect. This means cutting out what this specific person doesn't need or care about and highlighting *only* relevant information that applies to that person or situation while generating a feedback loop with the prospect.

Facilitating also allows you to make it easy to constructively work through any concerns, questions, or objections. The Stop, Drop, and Roll strategy works well to defuse emotions and focus on what matters most when faced with concerns and objections.

Matching the solution to Them specifically and working through objections leads the conversation into the final step.

Step 5: Then Consolidate

The "close" is often the target within a sales system. While we want to convert more prospects, not every sales conversation ends in a buying decision. In collaborative sales, *every* conversation should end with closure, both for you and for them.

Then Consolidate is the last step of WIIFT. The objective of *Then Consolidate* is to secure the prospect's decision or commitment and to clarify the next step. A commitment to a decision or action at the end of every conversation helps you advance the sale more quickly and creates efficiency for follow-up actions and conversations.

Consolidating begins with a check for their readiness to make a decision. If the readiness check doesn't solicit the decision, it is followed with a specific recap of how your solution will impact them (their WiifTs), and then an invitation to commit to a decision.

Once a decision is verbalized, the key efficiency booster follows: identify the next steps for all parties—who is doing what by when and how.

Your success in *Then Consolidate* to secure a decision or commitment relies on how well you accomplished the *Investigate* and *Facilitate* steps. If you haven't captured value and discussed concerns, a decision or commitment to action will be elusive.

The conversation does end with closure—a final confirmation of expectations and a sincere, personalized closing statement.

WIIFT Intro Final Thoughts

The WIIFT systematic approach to collaborative sales conversations is your roadmap for reaching a successful closure every time. Each step is useful on its own and builds on the preceding one, making transitioning through each component of the conversation smooth. And if you don't achieve the desired outcome, each step can be dissected for study and application. I'll discuss this further in future chapters.

Robotic use of the WIIFT system is not the goal. It is not so specific and prescriptive that it removes individuality. Quite the opposite: it allows you to remain human first with flexibility for your style, niche, prospects, and situations. It is not a script, but a framework. With practice and personalization, these steps become so habitual that they are seamlessly connected into a fluid, meaningful, and logical conversation with your prospect.

The system allows you to remain genuine, to really be you, as discussed in Chapter 1. Think of it as the curbs along the side of the road that keep us safe and guide us to our destination yet leave room for us to maneuver within the lanes, even allowing for U-turns when necessary!

WIIFT is effective both in one-step sales processes and multistep processes. It is the guide for each interaction/conversation within your sales process.

And now you've had your introductory overview of the 5 steps of WIIFT®. Chapters 15 through 41 outline the specific *whats* and *hows* for each step, sprinkled with plenty of examples and best practices. To keep yourself genuine, adjust the steps and tools to best fit your style, company processes, and client types.

As noted, WIIFT is the center of the model and is central to your conversation. However, the 5 Steps are also surrounded by two Actions that are just as important, Prepare and Prove. You'll learn more about this "cocoon" in the next chapter.

CHAPTER 7

The Cocoon of the WIIFT® Conversation System

"Metamorphosis is the most profound of all acts."

—Catherynne M. Valente, *In the Night Garden*

Cocoons fascinate me. From the outside they aren't that exciting, but knowing what is going on inside is! Their purpose is to protect their content, to provide a safe environment for metamorphosis. And that's exactly what Prove and Prepare do for the WIIFT Sales Conversation System. They keep the conversation, and your opportunity, safe so you can emerge from the sales conversation with success!

Prepare to Succeed

Let's start at the foundation. Preparation is the groundwork that makes every element of your sales conversation the best that it can be. Preparation is critical to each and every conversation.

That's why *Prepare* is the foundation of the WIIFT® system in Graphic 3–1. Preparation is present in the *Wait* step, yet is highlighted by showing it as the support of the entire conversation!

Preparation is a habit and a skill set. The act of preparing is not difficult; it's more about discipline. There are two levels of preparation that significantly increase your probability of achieving the desired outcome:

1. Advance Prep on screen or paper to outline the conversation and

2. Active Prep, which is the mental prep immediately before the conversation to break your preoccupation with everything else and focus on this prospect and situation.

The levels of preparation will be covered more extensively in Chapters 15–19, which explore the *Wait* step.

Your input before and during the conversation significantly impacts the output or the results. The term "garbage in, garbage out" has stuck with me since I took computer programming classes in my MBA program. It's the same with your sales conversations—and if you do not *Prepare* with relevant, timely, intentional, and focused input, you can expect your output to reflect that.

Here's what Rob and Eric Tilson, of Tilson Financial Group, have to share with an example about preparation:

A prospect called in anonymously asking to meet in person at our office. We were able to qualify him enough to proceed with scheduling.

Our preparation needed to be thorough because this colder lead, not through a referral, is not normal for us. We prepared using a Quick Prep Tool to Investigate and Facilitate this first conversation to uncover his POWNs and deliver more value than he expected.

In the first meeting, it was clear that his biggest motivation was to determine whether he could retire. And we were prepared to offer a one-time project to address this. But using the flow of a WIIFT conversation, we uncovered that a one-time project plan would not help him as much as a long-term investment management relationship. We described the ongoing process thoroughly, now knowing he was a Reflector Tribal Type. We found he was willing to consider this service instead of a one-time project.

With this prep used as a guide, we were able to uncover an additional $250,000 the client was ready to invest as well.

During our preparation for the second meeting, we made a strategic adjustment to our sales process that would better suit him. We gathered all necessary input for the retirement project as usual but also prepared investment resources and a proposed contract to send to him to review before the final meeting.

By the second meeting, the prospect had reviewed all the information we sent him, and he came in fully informed and ready to deliver his already signed contracts, much to our surprise.

The outcome is that we transformed a one-time project prospect into a long-term investment management client. That is a $12,000 project to a $25,000+ annual fee difference. You can bet we are believers and vocal advocates of the power of preparation for ourselves and all other members of our firm.

Preparation is so important I've included a tool as well as many tips and best practices in Chapter 44 to help you prepare efficiently and effectively.

Prove the Value of You and Your Service

Prove is the umbrella over the WIIFT steps, reminding us that we must consistently prove ourselves and the value of our solution in each conversation throughout the entire sales process. This is not a one-time occurrence; value is assessed by your prospect throughout the entire relationship.

Value is a subjective aspect of any sale. And for financial services, the real value of what you are selling is determined by your prospect— not by you or industry marketing.

You do, though, play a major role in proving value to the prospect. Your ability to provide the right proof at the right time reduces fee concerns, service scope issues, and other concerns and objections.

Your Personal Value

The value your prospect receives is attached to *you*! The actual value your prospects will associate with the solution begins with their experience with *you*. Every action you take—or don't take—can provide a proof point of value to your prospects.

I've experienced this firsthand. For many years, I represented a training solution in which quality was compromised because updates were released before they were ready and company leadership changed several times. During these transitions, many of my long-term clients told me the reason they continued to use the solution, despite its shortcomings, was because they wanted to work with me.

I didn't truly understand the implications of this until I developed my own sales training course in 2008. While I was confident that I could sell it to new companies, I underestimated the value my current clients placed on working with me and the impact that had on their willingness to adopt the new course for themselves. In the first year, I was pleasantly surprised when several clients told me that if I believed the new course was going to provide the skill and behavior-changing value they needed, they were "in."

One decision-maker committed to implementing the new course with his international team without even seeing an outline of the materials. Another participated in an abbreviated preview of the course because of her company's sourcing protocol, but she knew in advance that she was going to say yes. She knew that if she worked with me, she would not have to worry or manage the process as tightly. She trusted me.

Only after both agreements were signed did I consider the ease of making the transition to the new course. Here was a firsthand experience of the power of the personal value I had provided for years.

For advisors, your online reputation, clients, and the process for reaching and scheduling time with you all come into play.

Pause and reflect on the extra value *you* have added to your services and for your clients. Whether you know it or not, this personal value may have led, or will lead, to rewards you are unaware of.

Each week I hear powerful stories from advisors about the extra value they deliver to their prospects and clients, such as:

- Mediating a family conversation around transfer of wealth with an impending death

- Visiting clients at their homes instead of having them come to the office

- Sending prepaid envelopes to make it easy to return documents

- Connecting the client to attorneys, CPAs, and other professionals for other POWNs

- Creating and sending a one-page action plan

- Sharing a "questions to ask a financial advisor" document to support prospects making a good decision as they talk with potential advisors

- Running scenarios for potential approaches to buying a property

🍂 Researching solutions to "life" situations that aren't financially related, including how to bail a grandson out of jail in a foreign country!

These may not seem extraordinary, but they provide a lot of value to the client. Don't underestimate the value you add to each sales conversation and to the prospect throughout the sales cycle. As Joe Morgan, CFA, CFP said, "I realized I could be me and add value from the first interaction on. I didn't have to wait until they were a client."

Metrics Count in Proving Value

Though proof begins with you, it doesn't end there. You need to prove the value of your solution and your company throughout the sales conversation and the relationship as well.

Proving the value of your service is essential at each stage of the sales process and cycle. Keep in mind that value is in the eye of the prospect and is more powerful when it is:

🍂 Relevant to the person and particular situation

🍂 Timely throughout the sales conversation

🍂 Specific with measurable data and detail if necessary

Providing proof isn't a "one-and-done" step. Incorporating a "value summary" in client meetings also helps keep the focus on the ongoing value as well.

While metrics of financial gain are harder to use when compliantly selling financial services, you can use other types of metrics: examples of tax strategy savings, a retirement decision that affected monthly income, recommendations for exercising equity comp, or any other specific situations where there was a monetary impact. I suggest compiling a list of examples and successes that you can use as needed.

As Michael Dell said, "Anything that can be measured can be improved." Find a way to measure the outcomes and value your clients receive.

* * * * *

A productive sales conversation is more probable when you follow the WIIFT System steps cocooned with proper Preparation and Proof. The next section of this book provides further details on the 5 steps of WIIFT, as well as tips and tools to further systematize your conversations and make every conversation count.

CHAPTER 8

Successfully Using the WIIFT System

Use these quick tips from me and other advisors as well. Enjoy these success stories to help you find success using WIIFT.

Tips for Making WIIFT a Success

🌀 Apply the *WIIFT* 5-Step Sales System as your guide—*Wait, Initiate, Investigate, Facilitate,* and *Then Consolidate*—to make each conversation the most productive it can be.

🌀 Focus on *WiifT* (What's in it for *Them?*) through each step to move you forward to the next step of your conversation predictably and logically.

🌀 *Prepare* for conversation success. Make the time to identify the objective of your conversation and how you will lead the information exchange focused on Them, not you or your solution.

🌀 *Prove* yourself and your solution. Provide relevant proof through your actions, follow-through, and appropriate information throughout your conversation and relationship with the prospect.

Success!

🖋 Joe Forish shared, *"I got 2 new clients by using the WIIFT process. It felt incredible to have them say yes! Using the concepts of this sales process [and learning] how to listen and then how to match my services with buyers' POWNs are incredibly valuable!"*

🖋 Jonathan Grannick, the San Diego advisor whose conversion increased from 26 to 60%, wrote that adopting collaborative selling and the WIIFT system allowed him to have *"a better mindset for sales: Collaborative, not adversarial. Consultative, not pushy. Along with reasonable expectations and honest/authentic intentions that show through to the person on the other end. [That and] having a step-by-step process (WIIFT) to follow in all my conversations led to more conversions. I crave a step-by-step process in all that I do. Having something to follow helps immensely."*

🖋 Sara Young, Founder of Live + Give Financial, shared this story of using most of the system and tools for a success early in her firm's launch: *"I used the Quick Prep tool in advance of a prospect meeting. I was prepared with questions to ask from all 4 Points and was able to reference my Quick Prep Tool (QPT) during the meeting to keep the conversation organized."*

"Particularly helpful was thinking through, the "What do I need to learn during this conversation?" and tailoring the questions in advance, as well as during the call, to stay on track.

"I had very low expectations, as this was a cold outreach from my website, and they indicated they had a very specific planning question they wanted answered, but through the conversation, we uncovered a lot of other aspects that would be helpful for them to get advice on and realized the value of a comprehensive plan.

"*I also was able to more effectively close the conversation and leaned into asking about next steps. I realized she might be ready to make a decision right away based on what I had potentially identified as her Tribal Type in advance (Achiever), and sure enough—I pivoted from 'I'll send you an agreement to look over' to 'Would you like to move forward?' And she did!*"

CHAPTER 9

Tribal Types

"Dealing with people is probably the biggest
problem you face, especially if you are in
business. Yes, and that is also true if you are
a housewife, architect or engineer."

—Dale Carnegie

Stop Communicating the Way YOU Like

People are complex. This complexity makes any system or approach that involves people sometimes laughable! What works well in conversations and relationships in one situation may implode in another.

And that makes your selling, serving, and life so rich and interesting! How boring it would be if everyone else was just like us.

Your approach and actions surrounding personal connection, language choices, and pace matter. Have you noticed how some people need you to explain and describe every nitty-gritty detail of your recommendations and service? While others only want a high-level overview. Others have no real interest in your personal situation; they focus only on what you can do for them. Still, others want to be your new best friend, and the agenda or important decisions at hand can wait. And some people seem to need assurance and supporting data before they will do or decide anything.

Though the WIIFT Sales System is easily learned, the quality of its effectiveness is significantly impacted by you and the person in the conversation with you. That's why it needs to be adjusted for each individual and situation when used "in the wild," as I like to say.

But how? How do you provide what *they* want or need in each conversation? These efforts can be frustrating, time-consuming, and potentially revenue-defeating. That's why we need a shortcut! A way to quickly understand how to identify and then adjust to different types of people.

Of course, understanding people's unique behaviors or personalities is not a new concept; many models and assessments exist. I have used and am certified in several of them, including the Myers Briggs Type Indicator (MBTI), Social Styles, and DISC. Maybe you've been introduced to Caliper, the colors, animals, or any of a variety of personality assessments.

I appreciate the depth and the research behind them, and each model is helpful, yet I found a big gap in each one. After decades of introducing and using these tools, I found that it can be cumbersome, difficult, and even weird if you ask prospective clients to complete a 20-minute questionnaire on their style of communication. Oh, and then you have to remember many different personality-type combinations and quickly recall the information on the spot.

That's why we need a shortcut, an in-the-moment tool, to identify and adapt to the "customs" or connection, working style, and communication preferences of others while we are in the conversation.

Introducing Tribal Types

And that's where the Tribal Types model becomes valuable. It's an "in-the-moment" tool that supports your ability to quickly identify and then adapt to easily identifiable "customs" to help you work with and sell with people *in that moment.*

The word "custom" is important to understanding Tribal Types. A custom is defined as "an established practice, action, or thought process used by someone or a group of people."[4]

Customs are not only about what is innate or natural to people. They are practices that have been learned and adopted. And think about your prospects: they have practices and learned behaviors that they employ when they are in a "buying" situation. Their past experiences, negative connotations around selling (especially in financial services), and their fears come into play, often more than their personality or birth preferences.

When we work with people, their natural tendencies and preferences matter, of course. Yet in the selling process, we need to consider their past experiences and beliefs because they affect how the prospect shows up for our sales conversations. These are their customs.

By identifying their Tribal Type, you can focus on what they need *now* to be comfortable and committed to making the important decision to work with you.

Why *Tribal* Types? The name emerged when I was traveling in Brazil for work in 2008. My travel guide, Marcio, described groups of people with similarities as tribes. We were visiting Copacabana beach in Rio de Janeiro, and Marcio mentioned being aware of the different tribes before settling in. The *tribes*, or groups of people— teenagers, families, and singles—had similar customs and congregated together in specific areas each weekend. Their shared customs included communication styles, lifestyle preferences, and so much more!

I built upon my Brazilian experience and knowledge of personality and preference models and added the customs component to design the Tribal Types model. This model is a game changer according to many hundreds of advisors!

---

[4] Merriam-Webster online, s.v., "custom," accessed April 2024, https://www.merriam-webster.com/dictionary/custom.

To make the Tribal Types model easy to remember and, more importantly, easy to use, I've identified four distinct tribes. Of course, people are much more complex than four sets of tribal customs can explain, but with these four Tribes as a guide, you are well-equipped to make the necessary adjustments to converse effectively with most people.

This chapter will explain the Tribal Types model. The next chapters will introduce the four Tribal Types (*Achievers, Commanders, Reflectors,* and *Expressers*) followed by specific information for identifying each Tribe as well as strategies for selling and collaborating with them.

Additional information and how-tos for working through each step of the WIIFT Sales System with each of the four Tribal Types will be included in their respective chapters.

Tribal Types®

Graphic 9-1

The Tribal Types model, Graphic 9-1, illustrates several important points about Tribal Types:

🖢 The Tribes overlap in customs and behaviors and are displayed in open arcs vs. closed circles or boxes.

🖢 The words that begin on the tip of the inner arcs identify a key focus for the Tribes on either side. For example, a focus on results is associated with both the Achiever and Commander Tribes.

🖢 The middle of the model—the purple windmill-looking image— is the Neutral Zone. This is important! Starting each interaction within this zone allows you to switch directions and adjust quickly to the applicable Tribal Type customs. Neutral is often the safest place to start; from there, you can observe and then adjust your words, pace, and focus in the moment.

Using Graphic 9-1 as your guide, I suggest you read the descriptions of the four Tribal Types in the following chapters. Look for the patterns of customs in people you know and have worked with. You'll be able to easily identify people in the different Tribes.

Starting to Use Tribal Types

To use the Tribal Types information effectively, first identify your own Tribal Type. This personal awareness allows you to determine how you normally operate and communicate. Why? Because most of the time we operate in the way that is most natural and comfortable for us. And that can be a negative as my colleague Peter experienced.

When Peter, the president of a small company, was introduced to the model, he said, "If I assume that 25% of the population falls into each of these four Tribal Types, this means that for 48 years I have potentially been working and communicating with people incorrectly 75% of the time."

What an observation! How true this may be. If you are consistent in your own preferred customs when it comes to your selling style, working practices, conversations, pace, and detail orientation, you may be miscommunicating and working with people less effectively than you could be 75% of the time!

The Tribal Types descriptors and tips will help you determine the necessary adjustments you can make so your conversations are relevant and helpful to each prospective client. These adjustments will vary by person and situation.

You may need to slow down in your approach, provide more or less detail, be more open to personal connection, or prepare more substance or facts.

After introducing the Tribal Types model to advisors, I've heard some say, "I guess I can *act* like I'm _____." You can fill in the blank with: "interested in them," "just like them," or "caring." Acting is NOT the intention of a Tribes model. The model is to help us:

- Understand that not everyone is like you
- Identify different ways people communicate and work and the value they need from you
- Adjust how you work, communicate, and sell with them by speaking the same language and adapting to, acknowledging, and appreciating their customs

Identifying Tribal Types

I've included a simple Tribal Types Tool in Chapter 44 for identifying a person's Tribe. Begin using the Tool with yourself, and do not prejudge your Tribe without using the Tool. The specific descriptor selections in the Tool may identify a surprise or two for you! The more you use this Tool, the easier you can identify and adapt quickly to the customs of others to sell and collaborate with your prospects efficiently and effectively.

To identify Tribal Types in real time, observe all the clues—the *descriptors shown at the top of each column in the Tool Focus: Observed and Words Used.* The clues can be visual or audible. If your conversations are telephone-based, pay close attention to the audible nuances such as pace, word choice, tone, and level of detail they use. It is amazing what clues are present when you look and listen for them.

Identify if you need to slow down or speed up the conversation. Listen for the thinking or feeling words your prospect uses and adjust how you ask questions, paraphrase their concerns, and explain information accordingly.

Look for the level of personal connection they offer and seek. Think about their handshake, their eye contact, and the topics they bring up in your Connection Questions (you'll learn about these in Chapter 14).

In written correspondence, notice if they use full sentences and a personal, warm greeting or not. Ever get an email typed entirely in the subject line? Often that's a custom of Achievers, who think this saves them time.

As you practice identifying and adjusting, you'll begin to notice the nuances of each Tribe, allowing you to adjust more specifically.

How do I know this? A while back, I requested an Achiever's phone number via email. She replied, "It's in the Subject line." I missed that detail in her previous email because of the way my screen displays messages. This email was a clue to how this individual works: quickly and without a lot of details.

In written correspondence, notice that some people are friendlier with a sentence or two of small talk at the beginning of their email message. This is a clue for you to engage with them in the same way in your response.

It will take effort and energy to adjust to the different Tribal Types' customs—especially if they are the opposite of you. The good news is that in longer-term relationships, I've observed that most people will begin to blend their customs in working together. But beware: under stress or tight deadlines, they will quickly revert to their preferred customs, and you need to be ready to adapt.

So, where do you start to identify Tribes in your conversations and relationships? The **Neutral Zone** is at the center of this model. It's the starting place for any interaction. Start by actively observing everything you can. Starting from a place of neutrality allows you to quickly switch directions to make the necessary "in the moment" adaptations.

 TIMELY TIP

You will find that people pick up customs from their occupations, relationship dynamics, and environment.

🖋 They also take on "buyer behavior" customs when meeting with you for sales conversations.

🖋 They adapt their customs to get what they need, how they need it.

🖋 They also use them to make decisions and sometimes to make sure they aren't being taken advantage of.

As your conversations continue with the same people, you may find their actual preferred customs are different than your first impression of them.

That is why the Neutral Zone is the safest place to begin each conversation. From there, you can quickly adapt to the customs that are important to them at that time.

Understanding and applying Tribal Types has accounted for more converted prospects and stronger relationships than I can possibly mention here. My participants regularly report successes they attribute to their identification of and adjustments for Tribal Types.

For example, Ryan Gomez sent me this note:

"I allowed a Reflector the time to gather all the information he needed (including eleven separate documents and a supplementary cover letter) on our firm and financial planning process. He eventually agreed to wire us $1,850,000 for us to help manage."

He then shared that this was a Win[3] as the new client will be well taken care of, the firm has more AUM, and Ryan will earn a nice bonus.

That's what it can do for you!

Are you ready to meet the Tribes? We'll start at the top of the model and work clockwise in these next chapters: Achievers, Commanders, Reflectors, and Expressers. If you want to remember the four Tribes, think "ACRE."

CHAPTER 10

Meet the Achievers Tribe

"It is time for us all to stand and cheer for the doer, the achiever—the one who recognizes the challenges and does something about it."

—Vince Lombardi

Tribal Types®

Achievers are generally easy to pick out. They are high energy, quick, impulsive, and always on the move. They can be abrupt, confident, independent, and impatient, and they are often fast talkers. Achievers'

workspaces may appear cluttered and messy, but they can usually find what they need. They can seem dominating in their actions and conversations in their quest to get things done.

Achievers fear loss of respect or power, wasted time, or falling behind. It is not uncommon to see (or feel) their energy; they are often tapping a foot or jiggling their legs.

Buying Customs of Achievers

Achievers will want the sales process to move quickly. They may have enough information from their research before your conversation or, if it was a referral and they trust the referral source, were 85% ready to buy upon first connection.

You'll find they dislike an abundance of paperwork, details, and meetings. They will push you for information before you're ready to share it and may make a quick decision before you ever imagine they could … or should.

Now, if there is a good reason, you can slow them down, but it can be hard for them to stop suddenly when they are in motion. Like a fast-moving train, it takes them a while to slow down, stop, or change direction. Achievers are generally open to other ideas, but if you catch them in mid-motion, it may take a while for them to hear you or notice that there is a benefit to a different path.

If they are part of a couple, and the other spouse/partner is not an Achiever, they may drive the entire conversation and not give the other person an opportunity to participate in a significant way.

Working Style

Achievers have many goals and priorities. They also like to talk about their past achievements. Often, they expect things to get done at top speed. Because they work quickly, they assume others must as well. However, a change in plans won't usually bother Achievers, as they are used to adjusting their priorities often.

Despite their independence and confidence, Achievers want credit for what they accomplish. While some Achievers enjoy public appreciation and others prefer private, they all like their achievements to be acknowledged.

Word Choices

The words you will hear from Achievers include:

Effectiveness	Quick
Efficiency	I think this
Results	What have my peers done?
Time	Tell it like it is

Their conversations will focus on results, achievements, answers, and bottom lines. Achievers like to "tell it like it is," and while this candidness is helpful, it can also be seen as abrasive.

Level of Detail

A low level of detail is the norm with most Achievers. They only need quick, high-level concept overviews before they're ready to accept and act on them. Their movements might seem premature, but they like things to keep moving. They have been known to skip steps or details to reach a result more quickly.

Value that Achievers Want from You

Achievers find value in someone who can help them produce results efficiently and without distractions. They appreciate administrative and detailed work completed for them. They also like opportunities to be first or to try something new, and they value high-profile connections. Though they often tell you what they want from you, self-diagnosing and identifying the solution they think they need, they appreciate someone who is strong enough to clarify options or to push back to make something even better or quicker.

Strategies for Selling and Working with Achievers

- Use bullet points in writing and in your speech. Plan to be concise and prepare materials with high-level information. Achievers don't want to be bogged down with a ton of information or extra words. They want you to "net-net" ideas, suggestions, and questions.

- Be prepared to move to the next step quickly. Send materials in advance. Have necessary papers and next-step information readily available, but don't bring it out or complicate the conversation unless the information is needed for a specific reference. Achievers don't want extra stuff or information. Be ready to provide it when they ask for or need it.

- Always ask about time. Acknowledge and confirm the meeting will stick to the allotted time. Find out how much time they have allotted for your conversation. Even if you have scheduled 30 or 60 minutes, you may find them hoping it will only take half that time. While some say it is dangerous to allow Achievers to define conversation time, they may be more distracted by not knowing how long they will be with you.

🖋 Discuss their priorities first. Ask what they want to achieve near the beginning of the meeting.

🖋 Adjust to their pace. This does not mean you have to rush and match their pace. It means to show more energy and intensity and, yes, to increase speed. However, often you will need to help Achievers slow down a bit to cover necessary material. They may find this frustrating. Your ability to explain why they need to slow down or back up and to communicate the WiifTs is critical to gaining their time and attention.

🖋 Explain your intent or why specific details will be important to them. While it is important to reduce and take care of details for them, such as completing paperwork or reducing the number of options they should consider, don't skip what you know is necessary information. Use results and outcomes when describing benefits. Words like "efficiency," "results," and "effectiveness" are powerful Achiever words.

🖋 Compliment Achievers for their accomplishments. Sincerely acknowledging their successes or asking about them often gets them talking as much as Expressers. Adjust your mindset from "we accomplished this" to "you achieved this." Be careful not to make them feel bad about what they've done/not done in the past.

🖋 Meet all deadlines—the old "under promise and over deliver" mantra is helpful. However, note that if you accomplish something before a deadline, that shorter time frame will be their new expectation of you going forward.

🖋 Don't waste Achievers' time. Don't chitchat. Be brief, get to the point quickly, and be decisive. Finish early if possible.

🖋 Stay on topic and don't be insulted if Achievers abruptly cut you off to move things along.

- Provide only the most viable choices for Achievers to select from. This allows them to "net" out their options quickly. They don't want a long document or list of all the options; they value that you will short list the options to their best choices.

- Outline the next steps, making sure they are actionable and are getting something done.

- Don't waste their time by sharing details about the process.

- Provide plenty of reminders.

- Anticipate their needs and look for ways to save them time and add value.

While it's important to adjust to an Achiever's interest in details and their need for speed, it can lead to headaches further down the road. A wonderful client of mine, who was the leader of her firm's training initiative, is an Achiever. Because I was referred by several advisors from several firms she knew, the sales process was fast, and I needed to provide little detail.

After getting the yes to a firm-wide Genuine Sales® engagement, I insisted I needed time with the founder. I was told that would be impossible. When I said that the initiative wouldn't be as successful without syncing with the founder, I was told it wouldn't be necessary.

So, she and I worked on logistics: scheduling travel, organizing a 3-day workshop, selecting the advisors who would participate, and much more. I'd scheduled 45 minutes to work out these logistics, and we were done in 20 minutes.

While this time savings was great, it came back to haunt me. A few days before the training was to start, I finally had a conversation with the founder, which left me scrambling. Why? The founder and the leadership team *now* wanted details about why certain aspects of the initiative were important and had been scheduled in a certain way.

That led to a lot of last-minute changes and extra work to accommodate the seemingly "simple adjustments" they requested.

While I, as a fellow Achiever, was up to the challenge of the changes, it led to a couple of late nights. I should've known better and made sure that the meeting took place much sooner, and that we slowed down and got more specific so there wasn't so much scrambling.

Success!

A referral came in from an existing client. I immediately gave her a call to learn more about her goals and to qualify her as a prospect.

She stated how good her investment returns have been because of her stock picking in her roughly $2.5M portfolio. Even though she works with an advisor, she doesn't trust him and continues to do most of her own investing.

Right off the bat, she was a clear Achiever and results driven, but her mentioning not trusting her current solo advisor gave me an opportunity to inquire further. She shared that the advisor is unresponsive and when she asked for retirement projections, he just never did them.

I was able to convert this problem into what we could do to help her plan for retirement through our cash flow projections while also highlighting our team approach.

She was interested to learn more, and we scheduled the second meeting for the following week.

—JOE ORFF, WEALTHSTREAM ADVISORS

CHAPTER 11

Meet the Commanders Tribe

"Details matter. It's worth waiting to get it right."

—Steve Jobs

Tribal Types®

The Commanders Tribe are reserved and controlled in their speech and body language. They may fold their arms across their chest and often make direct eye contact. Their facial expression or tone is typically hard to read, though this doesn't mean they aren't emotionally connected to their situation or a solution. They are planners and analyzers who are precise, orderly, serious, and methodical.

Commanders' workspaces and homes are extremely organized. Their folders and filing systems are set up logically for the way they work. "Everything in its place" may be their motto. They tend to be conservative dressers and use more formal language. They are practical, diligent, and persistent, and they like to solve problems.

Common fears for Commanders include missing something, being wrong, losing, emotional reactions, and being criticized.

Buying Customs of Commanders

Commanders can be tough buyers. They want information backed by proof. They will potentially ask more questions than you, and they may want to drive the agenda.

They will have completed advance research and will likely vet several advisory options. Commanders will not value a personal connection, at least not at first. They will appear "all business" as they collect the information they need to make their decision.

Commanders are comfortable challenging facts and ideas. This doesn't mean they can't take in new information that contradicts their research, but they will not shy away from asking tough questions before accepting it.

Working Style

Commanders are analytical, logical, orderly, and systematic, and their decisions are fact-driven. They are competitive and like to "win" with their ideas and actions. Taken to the extreme, they can be seen as bureaucratic. They are planners and can be critical of others' planning (or lack thereof). Commanders do not need a lot of social interaction and often prefer agenda-driven meetings without a lot of small talk. This does not mean they are not interested in you. Once the agenda is taken care of, they will often engage in more personal conversation if there is extra time. That's a clue you have done well!

Commanders are usually very prompt and become irritated when others are not. They will ask for calendar invitations, pay very close attention to details, and want specifics for any requests for information and deadlines. They may bog down decisions with analysis and strive for accuracy, and they will spend extra time to "get it done right," and expect you to do the same.

Word Choices

Commanders' language is more formal and includes "thinking" words.

Why	How do you know?
Review	What proof is there to support that idea?
Compare	What's the primary source?
Validity	Research shows
Analyze	Is that your opinion or a fact?
Logic	
Control	

Level of Detail

Commanders prefer a high level of detail and expect accuracy. They will find the typos in your materials and point them out to you as a way of being helpful. They will review details over and over and want to know how information was calculated, determined, or secured. The accuracy of the data is as important as the depth and quantity.

Value that Commanders Want from You

Commanders know what they want. They have generally completed their own research, and their first questions may be about your knowledge and experience. However, this is where things can get off track when advisors start telling their whole story; Commanders don't want the whole story. They want only the requested pertinent facts.

Commanders will often test advisors at the beginning of a relationship to ensure they can trust their information and proposed solutions. The testing comes through challenging questions or ideas.

Since they want substantive information and an organized approach to the sale, relationship, service, and solution, they look for an advisor who is accurate and can help them make the right decision in a logical, organized way. Commanders want to be involved in all decisions related to their situation, and their ideas and opinions need to be acknowledged. They like the pros and cons of each option to be presented to them for analysis.

Strategies for Selling and Working with Commanders

🖋 Prepare a coherent and concise conversation with supporting information and agenda before the scheduled meeting time. Ask for a Commander's input on the agenda either before or at the beginning of the conversation to get buy-in. Ask for feedback about anything they want addressed.

🖋 Stick to the agenda unless you ask for permission to deter from it. Commanders may want to put your new ideas or information on hold until they get through what they want to discuss.

🖋 Prepare more information and details (hard data, facts, and research) in writing as backup—supporting data is always good! Commanders will analyze all information, so be prepared to show them the proof behind the data if you are questioned. They value primary source documentation. And make sure you proofread and review your materials.

🖎 Have visual aids and support items ready.

🖎 Be ready to explain the alternatives.

🖎 Don't be overly friendly or too personal at first. Commanders are not people to hug or double handshake. A firm and formal approach works best.

🖎 Keep your conversations fact-focused at the start and follow their lead in the level of personal talk. Use examples with facts versus stories with descriptions. Essentially, be concise and eliminate any fluff.

🖎 Practice what you'll say and speak directly and in clear language.

🖎 Develop a logical, well-structured presentation that explains the "why."

🖎 Get permission to offer suggestions and counterpoints.

🖎 Set realistic deadlines. Ask Commanders for a realistic time frame and confirm deadlines before ending your conversation.

🖎 Don't work from your opinion or gut instinct. Base your actions and decisions on facts, not theory or speculation. And be ready to prove your details.

🖎 If there is a problem or objection, ask for the Commander's help to address it.

🖎 Give Commanders the opportunity to show their problem-solving abilities. Ask them how they have completed or addressed similar situations in the past.

🖎 Follow up your conversations with a short, written summary and confirmation of next steps and time frames. Provide expectations of results and timeline.

And don't fret: even if you think you "blew it" with a Commander, they may still move forward with you, as evidenced in a challenge with a Commander I experienced early in my career. When I first met Philip, after two easy and fantastic conversations with an Expresser manager on his team, he directed me to my seat in the conference room—directly across the table from him.

He told me what the agenda was and in what order he wanted information from me. He shared specific details on his problems and what he thought he needed in a sales training solution. At one point he even reached across the table and took my notepad to review the notes I had been writing. He mentioned he wanted to make sure I was capturing his intent "correctly." Thankfully, he concluded I had taken accurate notes.

The next step was a presentation to his management team. It went so well, he suspected that we had manipulated them in some way. The other managers remained positive though, and he kept moving forward in the buying process.

Further in the sales process, I was not reading his signals that it was time to ask him for a decision, and he finally said, "Nancy, I'm going to do your job for you; we are ready to implement this training."

Fortunately, despite the rough start, I delivered what was promised, kept this individual's needs in mind as we worked with his team and provided factual updates each week, and even slowly learned more about him as a person. I must have done something right because when he moved to a new company, he sought my services there as well.

Success!

We had a prospect, who we met at a wine event. Started off very standoffish, but I went back to Tribal Types and knew that I was dealing with a Commander. Steered the conversation to be more direct to him by asking the right questions and getting straight to the point. The prospect thoroughly enjoyed that, and we were able to get the next meeting scheduled.

At that meeting, we then built a rapport and ended up finding the right solution for him, and he became a client.

—NICK, KY

CHAPTER 12

Meet the Reflectors Tribe

"Without reflection, we go blindly on our way,
creating more unintended consequences,
and failing to achieve anything useful."

—Margaret J. Wheatley, American writer and teacher

Tribal Types®

Reflectors are cooperative, friendly, patient, agreeable, good listeners, and people-focused. They may not show a lot of outward physical energy; they will appear more reserved than others and will not seek attention in a crowd.

Often, they stand on the fringe in group situations to observe the dynamics, situation, and people before contributing. They are often quiet—not because they are meek, but because they do not need to call attention to themselves. When you ask a Reflector a question, they will pause for what may seem like a long time before responding. They prefer to think their answer through before stating it out loud. You will find that Reflectors enjoy being a part of a team if it is cohesive and if each person carries their weight.

Reflectors become frustrated when their opinion is overlooked or they aren't asked to participate in high-profile activities. Yet they often don't raise their hand first, not because they are less interested, but because they want to think before volunteering.

Reflectors fear missing something, breaking rules, and losing security or stability. They also fear change and the unknown.

Buying Customs of Reflectors

Reflectors are careful buyers. They want clearly explained information and processes, with the details in writing. They'll want to know your background and what drove you to this business. Reflectors may want to know about, and possibly talk with, people you've worked with who they consider to be "like them."

Often Reflectors will not even talk to you until they have screened you, reviewed all the information they can find online about you, and checked out your ADV. They may want to confirm this information when they meet with you.

While you may not secure a decision on the spot, if you provide a caring experience, the information they need, and guidance on time-lines, a decision will come. And it will stick.

Working Style

You will find that Reflectors are careful in their approach. They may ask a lot of questions before agreeing to or beginning new activities. Reflectors are precise and thorough. There is no rushing them; the stress of pressure may even slow them down and surely frustrate them. They are not your first adopters of ideas or actions. They are process- and policy-focused, and they will find any holes in them. Reflectors don't like any steps to be missed or skipped by anyone.

In meetings, Reflectors often will not be the first to express a new idea or to volunteer information. They will wait for their opinion to be solicited. If it isn't, they may show annoyance later or say, "Well, no one ever asked me."

Word Choices

They are diplomatic in their speech and careful with their word choices. When taken to the extreme, this can be perceived as weak or wimpy, though it isn't.

The words you will hear from Reflectors include:

How	When should … ?
Feel	This is how we do it
Process	Don't want to rush through this
Order	Are you sure?
Structure	Who else?
Careful	Has that worked before?

Level of Detail

Reflectors pay attention to details. They prefer a high level of detail shared when you describe anything to them, and they will review notes or recall details and know where to get any necessary data. They will create reference information for themselves and for everyone else to document the process and keep everyone following it.

Value that Reflectors Want from You

Reflectors value a logical and consistent approach to situations. They like information in advance and want to know the steps and who will be involved. Reflectors appreciate an advisor who guides and supports their efforts without overt pressure. They appreciate being given all the information and time they need to make a decision. However, they do appreciate a timeline for a decision to be made, as it helps them finalize their decision. They value good listeners because they are good listeners.

Strategies for Selling and Working with Reflectors

- Talk at a normal pace. Don't talk down to Reflectors or speak so slowly that they feel you think they are slow. They aren't less intelligent!

- Ask if anyone else should be involved in the conversation.

- Give plenty of info about the meeting logistics.

- Share your intent and context with Reflectors before asking questions. Then pause for up to 20 seconds (gasp!) while they first mentally process their response and listen. Do not rush their answers. It will be worth the wait! As they respond, don't interrupt; let them complete their sentences and thoughts.

- Ask questions and share opinions without being too aggressive. Though Reflectors need assistance and some assertiveness, do not be too pushy or demanding on timelines and final decisions.

Plan enough time in your conversations to review details, answer detailed questions, and allow Reflectors to explore options.

🍂 Help Reflectors make decisions by asking for reasonable deadlines. Ask how much time they need to examine the information and offer your assistance in reviewing options and details. If they ask for more time than you feel is needed, ask if there is any way it could be done to fit a shorter time frame.

🍂 Provide an agenda and questions to review in advance of your conversation. Reflectors will take the time to review and prepare their responses. This will save time during your conversation and help you provide more thorough information.

🍂 Value Reflectors for who they are. Ask about them and their family to build rapport. Let them know the relationship matters by connecting with them personally before jumping into your agenda. They want to know about you and whether they can trust you, which alleviates any fears or concerns they have. This will help them be more open during your conversation.

🍂 Share specifics and details about how your service works and the process you will work through with them. Let Reflectors know exactly what happens after they make a decision.

🍂 Be ready to talk about details and processes. Have a process and stick to it. If something does deviate, explain why, giving the rationale for any changes.

🍂 Give Reflectors opportunities to meet others on your team when possible. This provides a sense of security and familiarity with a backup if you aren't available.

🍂 Encourage Reflectors to make suggestions and share their opinions. They are generally observant and may have an idea no one else would have thought of. Often this information will not be volunteered unless it is asked for.

🖋 Invite them to reach out and ask follow-up questions afterward and allow them the opportunity to get feedback from others. Don't rush the decision; instead, give them the chance to do their own research.

🖋 Keep in mind that security is important to them, so be consistent and follow through with words and actions.

Reflectors can be fantastic clients. I have had the privilege of working with Laura, a Reflector for over 4 years. Laura appreciates that I give her information in advance of our planning calls. She is always prepared and likes to collaborate and talk through ideas before we commit to them.

Laura's follow-up information is also precise and well thought out. As a leader in the firm, she is very good at tracking details and setting specific expectations. She appreciates the additional conversations we have that relate to her in more than just her sales role.

I have found that when I wait and let Laura process her ideas or responses without interrupting, her responses are always very valuable.

Success!

I identified a prospect's Tribal Type as a Reflector, so I geared the conversation towards their Tribe. I did a lot of prep work for the meeting and even created a document which showed which slides to present when—made me feel very confident going into the meeting.

I also reviewed this information the night before so I had a good idea of their Tribal customs. I knew I was going to have to carry a lot of the early conversation, so I had a list of questions prepared to ask them.

The question that helped me the most and where they offered the most information was "What do you see my role being if I worked with you?" I had in big letters on my desk during the meeting the phrases: "PAUSE," "So if I understand you correctly," and "SLOW down the conversation"—this helped me from interrupting and also kept me from rushing through the meeting.

The end result was that the couple signed up as a client with a fee of $19,000. I do not believe this would have been possible had I not taken the Genuine Sales® course to learn how to sell collaboratively.

—JOHN MUNLEY, WHEALTH ADVISORS

CHAPTER 13

Meet the Expressers Tribe

"Be who you are and say what you feel
because those who mind don't matter
and those who matter don't mind."

—Unknown

Tribal Types®

Expressers are energetic, sociable, and talkative. They will "work the room" and talk to many people. They may appear to be disorganized and indecisive, yet that doesn't mean they are. They talk a lot about personal things and want to know how you feel.

Expressers seem to know everyone, or at least they want to, and networking is important to them. Their emotions are often very visible; some might even say they wear their heart on their sleeve. Expressers fear earning bad reputations, disappointing others, becoming outdated, being rejected, and not being valued as a person.

Since Expressers tend to be trendy dressers and don't mind clothes that call attention to themselves, they are the person wearing holiday ties and scarves! They are animated talkers and use their body language to add color and content to their conversation. You may notice they use emojis and exclamation marks in their written messages.

Buying Customs of Expressers

Expressers are often very engaged in each conversation throughout the sales process. They will share all the information you ask for, plus more! Their experience with you will significantly contribute to their confidence in working with you. They especially want to know that *they* matter to you.

They seek input from others before making decisions. They often ask friends, family, and other advisors for their opinions on fee structures, services, and advisors. They can sound like they are moving forward and then back off after the fact. They will not want to deliver "bad" news to you face-to-face.

Working Style

Expressers are people-focused and prefer a consensus for activities, decisions, and workflow. Their decisions are swayed heavily by the impact the outcome will have on others. Sometimes Expressers come off as a little scattered to other Tribes because they want to explore and discuss all ideas and check in with everyone involved. They may implement new ideas or start new activities and then lose interest before they are completed.

They may work outside the established systems or processes to get things done through their connections. Expressers support their family and team members. They are demonstrative in their appreciation for others and appreciate recognition for who they are and their contributions to the team.

Word Choices

Expressers use stories and detailed descriptions when responding to questions. The information they provide is not always given in a straightforward linear path, and in its extreme, this may make the Expresser appear disorganized.

The words you will hear from Expressers include:

Who?	How are you?
Awesome	Do you like this?
Like	What do others say?
Happy	I love …
That's great	Will I work with you directly?
I feel	I'm feeling that …

Level of Detail

Expressers have lower attention to detail than the other Tribes. They prefer to focus on the big picture. They will not read or research pages and pages of information.

Value that Expressers Want from You

Expressers want to like their advisor. They value people they can connect with and who can help them navigate the decision-making process. Since they appreciate the opportunity to be first or to introduce something "new" to others, they are often first adopters of an idea if they like the people involved. Expressers appreciate an advisor who treats them well, provides personal attention, and helps them stay on track. They want loyalty and to be cared for as a person, not just as your prospect or client.

Strategies for Selling and Working with Expressers

- Prepare to spend more time in a conversation with an Expresser. This will allow for personal connections, stories, and tangents. Leave time at the beginning and end of the meeting for chitchat.

- Don't rush. Give them time to talk and express themselves.

- Be clear on the agenda to avoid being sidetracked but allow room for things to be more fluid and less structured.

- Prepare a relevant story or anecdote.

- Look for ways to connect ahead of time. Ex: Where they live, hobbies, shared interests, etc.

- Prepare questions and information through a lens of "feeling" that shows an interest in them and their situation. And when they answer, make them feel validated and understood.

- Be positive and upbeat. Convey genuine enthusiasm and excitement.

- Be more direct than with other Tribes to keep the conversation focused. By sharing intent and context with Expressers before asking a question, you'll help them respond with relevant information.

- If an Expresser's response is getting too long, it is okay to interrupt and redirect them. Apologize for cutting them off and then ask a new question or redirect as necessary.

- Pay attention to Expressers and offer genuine compliments, credit, and recognition. Don't dominate the conversation.

- Ask Expressers for their ideas, opinions, or suggestions. Then prepare to listen, as they will have a lot of them. Listen closely, as there are often good nuggets to be mined from the information.

- Remember special dates and events such as birthdays, work anniversaries, when they were on vacation, etc. This personal touch is especially important to Expressers.

- Take careful notes to document information and action items. Take care of as many details as possible since Expressers will not naturally keep track of them. Send a short, written follow-up with a summary of the details, commitments, and actions. Include a note on how happy you were to spend time with them and what you specifically appreciate about your conversation or them. Be prepared to follow up with them more than once.

- Invite others to the conversation to allow Expressers to get the consensus they prefer. Ask permission from the Expresser first, though, so he or she doesn't feel you are going over their head or lessening their importance.

- Develop the ongoing relationship—don't make it transactional.

- Provide a point of contact or direct line for them.

- When explaining your solution, use stories and anecdotes that are people-focused.

Expressers can be easy to work with, but they can be a challenge at the same time!

I have had the privilege of working with many high-energy Expressers in my business. One Expresser, a referral, connected personally with me on the very first phone call. By the second phone call, she was already my internal influencer to navigate the decision for her team.

Because of this client's ability to understand the people in each role, we were able to position the sales training for each decision-maker's needs. She had balanced her Expresser customs and was able to take care of the details and deliver on what was promised.

This client's association with me was important, and we enjoyed a fantastic 5-year working relationship providing great value to those on her team. Seeing her as a person first was just as important to my success as was the "real work" we completed. She advocated for me and my solution over and over again.

Success!

I had an Expresser prospect that I met randomly in our office building, and ended up having a two-hour meeting that, for the first time, I noticed I was truly aligned with the other person's POWNs and adjusted my communication and presentation to match what the client wanted and needed rather than what I wanted.

The Tribal Types have been a very important tool in my toolkit so that I am able to match the message to the audience rather than trying to force everyone to accept my own perception of what they want to hear.

–DAMIAN PALFINI, CAVALOT CAPITAL

CHAPTER 14

Tribal Types Quick Tips

Did you recognize yourself and others you work with as you read through the discussion of Tribal Types? There are many ways to collect information about a person's customs, traits, and habits if you observe the signs and clues they provide about what is important to them, how they want to work, and their preferences for communication. The value of the Tribal Types Tool, shared in Chapter 44, becomes evident when you use the information to communicate more effectively "in the moment."

One final comment about Tribal Types: People are, as I said at the beginning of the chapters on Tribal Types, much more complex than can be described in these four Tribes. You will find that some people are a delightful—or not-so-delightful—combination of several Tribes. The more you pay attention to the customs, the more you will notice unique combinations and the easier it will be to make the adjustments that count for that person.

Quick Tips for Using Tribal Types

🌀 Identify your own Tribal Type first. Acknowledge how you prefer to work and communicate. Identify how you make "buying decisions." This awareness will allow you to adjust as necessary from your normal actions when dealing with other Tribes.

🌀 Use the Neutral Zone. Top advisors are like chameleons; they easily adapt and work with different people in different ways. Start in the Neutral Zone with active observation to quickly identify how to work and communicate during each conversation. From there, adjust to the person's pace, language, and values that are relevant to their Tribal Type.

🌀 Remain flexible with your approach in each conversation. Don't judge or box in your prospective clients. The environment and the person's experiences in the previous 20 minutes will impact their behavior and communication in the first 20 minutes of your conversation. Every time you are in contact with someone, observe their communication customs—focusing on pace, word choice, and level of personal connection—and adapt.

🌀 Prepare for every conversation with the individual's Tribal Type in mind. Determine the information you should have available, the way you should word your questions, how much small talk to plan for up front, and the ways in which you should provide value. Then be flexible in the moment to ensure you are delivering what they need at that time.

🌀 Appreciate the uniqueness of each person. Some may be more challenging for you to sell to and collaborate with than others. Strive to provide value in each of your interactions.

PART II

The Whats and How-tos of Collaborative Sales Conversations

CHAPTER 15

Wait Step:
The Conversation Starts with You

*The shortest path to a successful
conversation starts with preparation.*

—A Nancy Timely Tip

Preparation: we all *know* it's important, yet how do we make it easy and efficient? How do we make the time for it? And is the time we spend prepping worth it?

Those are good questions about this extremely important step that kicks off the WIIFT® Sales System.

And the questions don't end there. The most common questions I hear are:

- *What should I prepare for?* A complete, collaborative conversation.

- *How much time should preparation take?* There is no exact time that is ideal. It could be 5 or 45 minutes. It depends on the situation.

- *Is it worth my time?* Yes! In a controlled study we conducted with a client, we found that every minute of prep created saved up to 1.7 minutes. How? The conversation was more efficient and productive. That productivity led to fewer follow-up activities afterward.

Let's look closer at this often-incomplete step of a WIIFT® collaborative sales conversation.

Who would think that your opportunity to convert collaboratively starts before the conversation? Well, if you are following the WIIFT Sales System, it does! What you do before entering the conversation does impact your ability and probability of collaboration.

Most advisors know they need to prepare and compile information to share, questions to ask, and, if possible, information about the prospect. What is missed, though, is the preparation for leading the entire conversation itself.

To increase your confidence and ability to lead a successful collaborative sales conversation, develop the discipline to *make time for the right type of preparation*. Notice I didn't say "take" time. Often, we need to *make* the time and prioritize our preparation as explained in these chapters.

The good news is that more effective preparation is completely in your control! Because *Wait* is the only step of WIIFT you complete before contacting your prospect, it's the ONLY step that you solely control. You either make the time for it or you don't.

As we move into the first step of WIIFT, you can expect to see Objectives (Whats) and Actions (How-tos) for every WIIFT® step, along with at least 4 chapters covering:

🖋 Introduction

🖋 "Anchor" that frames an easy, consistent, memorable approach for the step

🖋 Nuances that make your actions most effective

🖋 Best practices and quick tips for easy reference in the future.

Ready to get into it? Here we go! The *Wait* Step's overall objective is to maximize the time with the prospect. Yet there are additional objectives for this elevated type of preparation. Review the next page for the Objectives and the Actions/How-tos for this step of the conversation.

The Wait Step Overview

 Objectives

✓ Maximize the time with the prospect
✓ Break preoccupation
✓ Know your audience

When you make the time for the Actions of the Wait Step, you fulfill the main purpose of this step—a readiness to maximize the time with your prospective clients in a productive, value-filled conversation. To Wait successfully there are five Actions or how-tos:

 Actions/How-tos

1. Complete the Quick Prep Tool and appropriate research
2. Check your mirror and materials
3. Eliminate distractions
4. Review notes prior to conversation
5. Prepare your mind to engage with the prospect: Focus on the What's in it for Them (WiifT) for this conversation

The Actions outline the two levels of preparation necessary to gain the most benefit:

1. Advance Prep: In advance on screen or paper.
2. Active Prep: Immediately before the conversation and interactions.

For each step outlined in the book, you will find there is an "Anchor," a framework that provides a routine or mini-process for you to follow. This makes the steps memorable, so you can easily, consistently, and consciously put them into practice in your sales conversations.

The anchor to the *Wait* step is Preparation with Advance and Active Prep. In this chapter, you'll learn more about Advance Prep and the next several chapters will cover Active Prep.

Graphic 15-1

Graphic 15-1 shows how the 2 levels of preparation that highly increase your probability of a successful outcome are equally important to calibrate your plan for achieving a specific outcome in advance of your conversation.

The prep you complete in Advance of your conversation is important for ensuring that you have resources, others, and the prospective client prepped. And the Active preparation immediately before the conversation allows you to lead the conversation and be present.

Advance Prep Action 1: Complete the Quick Prep Tool and Appropriate Research

Prepare On Screen or Paper

Putting pen to paper or fingers to a keyboard allows you to outline the objectives, actions, and outcome for your conversation. As televangelist, speaker, motivator, and author Robert H. Schuller said, "Spectacular achievement is always preceded by unspectacular preparation."

You can easily prepare by using the Financial Advisor Quick Prep Tool I'm providing on the next pages. You can also download your own Quick Prep Tool (QPT) here.

The first page of the QPT will help you outline the conversation from start to finish. Please note that I purposely wrote "outline" and not "script." While scripts are useful in many situations, in a sales conversation, a script is only as helpful as to the extent your prospective clients are also following it, and we know they aren't!

Not only does Advance Prep outline the conversation, it allows you to complete the appropriate research that will increase the relevancy of what you focus on during the conversation. You can complete research for more than one conversation at a time and cluster your prep time to get the best information and resources lined up and prep the prospective clients, if possible. It will also help you keep the conversation focused on relevant information and solutions.

WIIFT **Quick Prep Tool**™
for Financial Advisors

Date: _____

Name (All names and roles, if applicable)　　　　　　Tribal Type©(s)

WAIT Objective(s) for conversation

Prospect's Need to know (plus POWNs if known)　　Need to knows (What I need to learn)

Value and benefits important to Them (How will I differentiate our solution?)

INITIATE 3-Step Start notes (Greet, Explain why, Ask time/connection questions to open)

NOTES

INVESTIGATE 4-Point Questions to uncover POWNs (Problems, Opportunities, Wants, and Needs)

Today　　　　　　　　　　　　　　　NOTES

Tomorrow

Risk

Reward

FACILITATE Possible recommendation(s) or information to be shared with Whats to WiifTs

NOTES

Possible objections or concerns with notes for
Acknowledge, Ask questions, Answers with WiifT
　Objections　　　　　　　　　Ask Questions

THEN CONSOLIDATE Decision or commitment desired and 3-Step Finish Notes
　　　　　　　　　　　(Check for Readiness, Confirm, Ask). Next steps and expectations to set

NOTES

Follow-up Action Items

What	Who	When	How

Graphic 15-2 presents the first page, WIIFT Quick Prep™

Quick Research™

Date: _____

Access research sources to help understand this prospect(s). Review any information collected from emails, CRM, online questionnaires, social networking groups, LinkedIn, company or industry forums, "Google" etc.

Research notes – Who are they? Where do they work? What's their presence online? Who are they connected with? Who is in their family? What do they do for fun? What types of groups or affiliations do they have?

For this prospect(s), what is in alignment with our services? What potential value do we offer?

What specific information do I need to qualify this prospect? Quantitative information: assets, income, career, family stage, etc. Qualitative information: willingness to change, take advice, collaborate, work with an advisor, pay for services, follow-through, personality fit, etc.

For a business prospect, use the following section to guide your research -

Review company's website, LinkedIn profiles of key people, brochures, annual reports, and marketing documents for useful information about:

Mission or value statement

Key stakeholders (names, roles, backgrounds)

Recent company business news (financial results, news releases)

Specific business goals (new markets, expansion, returns to stakeholders, personal goals, etc.)

Research the Situation and Person

The second page of the QPT, Quick Research, guides you through specific considerations to ensure your conversation is relevant to the prospect's current situation. It will help you find further opportunities and potential conversation points with the prospect.

This Quick Research page is best used in combination with online information you can easily access about your prospect. Begin with a search for the prospect's name in search engines to locate the social media sites and forums where they "hang out." Google, Facebook, LinkedIn, Instagram, and X are great starting points.

Please note: Internet searches do not make you a stalker. Most prospects appreciate that you are researching. The information you gather is only dangerous if you use it in a stalker-like way! Use the information to identify starter questions or look for people or affiliate connections. Don't say, "I saw your family's holiday photo. Your daughter is so beautiful!" That is stalker-talk!

Instead, use the information to form questions such as, "In prepping, I noticed your family photos online. What do you enjoy doing with your family for fun?"

If you are connecting on LinkedIn, the person will be notified that you (or "someone" if you don't have a premium account) have viewed their profile. Use this as an opportunity to send them a connection request with a note such as, "I am preparing for our upcoming conversation and found you here. I'd be honored to connect with you here. Looking forward to our conversation."

With the additional information you collect, begin identifying how your solutions align for the prospect as you fill out the Quick Research page. Identify the value you can offer to this person, couple, family, or situation so you can incorporate that information into every part of your conversation.

Prep the Prospect!

As you prepare to lead the conversation, identify ways you can prep your prospect.

Consider this: Most prospects don't know how to buy a professional service like yours. So, the more you can help them see the path forward and remove as much mental and physical effort on their end, the more present and focused they will be during the conversation.

To make your prospect's prep most efficient, create personalized templates to support this process. Set it up through your scheduling program if you have one, or send a prep email with information on logistics, dress, background of the firm, yourself, and/or your team, technology requirements, parking directions, meeting objectives, materials they should submit or prepare, and so on.

To determine the type of prep the prospect needs, ask yourself (or them) these questions:

- What do they need to know in advance to allow them to be more comfortable with the conversation and process?

- What materials can be shared in advance or brought with them? What should they think about ahead of time? What should they prepare to share in the conversation?

- How is the meeting being held? Video, phone, or in person? What instructions do they need to prepare to make the location or mode of communication most beneficial?

You can complete this Advance Prep hours or days before the conversation. Then, apply the second level of prep, Active Prep—covered in the next chapters—to prepare for leading the live conversation.

The benefits of using the QPT are best articulated by those who have used it over the past few years. These are actual comments from users:

"I have really gained value preparing for each of my calls. This has allowed me to have better conversations and has provided the prospect with a better solution."

"Doing the Quick Prep sheets makes it easier to focus on the conversation on hand and not scramble for the right words. It gives me the opportunity to focus on what the prospect is saying instead of worrying what to say next."

"Preparation has benefited me greatly. I now make sure to prepare myself ahead of time before I go into a sales call. This helps me to stay focused during the call and enables me to have more control during the sales process."

"Use of the Quick Prep Tool has enabled more efficient and effective meetings. Meetings are shorter and result in clear decisions being made."

CHAPTER 16

Wait Step:
Your Mirror and Materials

You, and anything your prospect sees, hears,
smells, or touches will impact their confidence
and commitment to working with you.

—A Nancy Timely Tip

The *Wait* Step's Advance and Active Prep continues with a look at the visuals! You, and anything your prospect sees, hears, smells, or touches, will impact their confidence and commitment to working with you.

What message do your prospects take away when they look at you and the materials you provide? Your appearance, body language, voice, and handouts all convey a message. Whether you are meeting in person, on video, or on the telephone, it's important to check your mirror and materials, which is Action 2 in the *Wait* step, before you engage.

Advance Prep Action 2: Check Your Mirror and Materials

This Action is a blend of Advance and Active Prep. Certain aspects can be done well in advance, and some need attention immediately before the conversation.

A Look at You

The first indication that you believe your prospects matter to you is made with your personal presentation. What's great now is the acceptance of all kinds of styles in financial services. It wasn't always so.

When I was in banking, our branch employees still wore uniforms. And our branch managers were to stand out by *not* being in uniform. Unbelievably to me, the branch managers pushed back on this! Yet we knew that customers were looking for the visual that showed who was "in charge." So, we took an expensive and drastic measure to boost their confidence and credibility: we hosted a day-long image event.

We brought in speakers who shared tips on dressing for success and on hair and makeup. Then we gave each participant a surprise cash bonus to put the tips into practice. The results were astounding. The managers carried themselves with more confidence and began establishing more credibility with the business clients. The board of directors declared it a wise investment.

Now, advisors have so many more options for what is acceptable to wear when meeting with prospects and clients!

Please don't ignore the tips that follow because you think that "everyone already knows this." You may just find a golden nugget that helps you present your best self.

For in-person meetings

🦞 *Dress according to your audience.* Kevin, an advisor who works with clients who have an ultrahigh net worth, would not dream of showing up for prospect meetings without dress pants, a button-down shirt, and sports coat. Others who work with a very different prospect can wear T-shirts or a polo and jeans.

🦞 *Don't forget your vehicle and office space.* If you meet your prospects in person, they may notice the condition and cleanliness of your vehicle. Your office space should also represent your level of professionalism, organization, and style.

🦞 *Ensure your breath and personal hygiene are odor-free.* Although this is common sense, you may be surprised by the stories prospects have shared with me about odors. Common complaints include heavy cologne, body spray, or perfume, as well as coffee breath and cigarette smoke odor. Take it easy on the sprays and ensure your breath is not offensive.

For telephone conversations

🦞 *Eliminate sounds around you whenever possible.* What the prospect hears is part of your personal presentation.

🦞 Organize any documents, whether paper or online, you may need, and have paper and a pen available to take notes. The sounds of shuffling papers and mouse clicking can make you appear unprepared or disorganized.

🦞 *Ensure your voice is clear and professional.* Clear your throat or have a drink of water before the call. Do not eat or chew gum. Callers can even hear if you are chewing on a pencil or sucking on a mint.

🦞 Test connection to reduce the potential of a bad cell phone connection. And gasp! Landline phones are still viable and more reliable!

⑨ *Don't drive and dial.* Tempting as it may be to return calls while on the road, it can also send the message that you are squeezing them in or that you are not focused (and in some states, it's illegal). Pull to the side of the road or into a parking lot before calling a prospect. If you use a headset, earbuds, or speakerphone, reduce the noises in your vehicle. If someone else is with you, let your caller know. If you aren't behind the wheel, have a pen and paper available for note-taking.

For video conversations

⑨ *Look the part.* Dress as if you were meeting in person.

⑨ *Create the right background.* Your background should represent your style and preferences. Ask someone in your circle of connections to check it out and provide feedback.

⑨ *Turn off your self-view.* When you don't have to look at yourself on camera, you will be less distracted and more focused on your prospects!

⑨ *Test your equipment.* Periodically ask team members, colleagues, or family members to have a video call with you and check the sound and picture quality. Conduct regular speed tests to make sure lagging isn't an issue.

Following these common-sense tips will help you look sharp and be ready to make a positive first impression that engages your prospect.

Determine the Right "Stuff" for Your Conversation

Any materials you share with your prospect, virtual or printed, represent the level of professionalism and quality that they will associate with you. So does the "stuff" you personally use—briefcase/backpack, computer, portfolio, marketing materials, and even your pen.

For years, I had a black laptop. I loved it, but unfortunately, the shiny black outer shell easily showed fingerprints. I didn't realize for a while how awful this looked to anyone sitting across from me, including a room full of training-course participants, nor did I think to wipe down my computer top before my presentations. Then one day, as I co-presented with a colleague, I noticed how sloppy the fingerprints looked. It reminded me that *all* my materials and equipment are an extension of my personal presentation and that they need to look clean and professional.

Evaluate the documents or items you will share with your prospects as you are collaborating to verify whether everything presents the image or message you want. To ensure your "stuff" represents you and your solution positively, first determine what you need for your conversation:

Brochures	Handouts
Technology-based visual aids	Paper, pen, and portfolio
A laptop or tablet	Branded items to share
Briefcase or backpack	

Then evaluate from the prospect's perspective whether each item presents the image you want. If possible, ask others for feedback. If it doesn't present a positive image or advance the credibility of you and your firm, adjust or eliminate it.

The "right" materials may be very different for each Tribal Type. For Commanders and Reflectors who like to "see and touch," you should print out information, supporting data, and a process layout. They appreciate tables, graphs, and detail. For Expressers and Achievers, the right material is less detailed, yet it needs to capture their attention. Simplify your message with a picture, simple model, or graphic to keep them focused.

CHAPTER 17

Wait Step: Active Prep to Stop Distractions

Eliminate your distractions, reduce the temptation to multitask, and make it easier to keep your conversation focused where it belongs: on your prospects.

—A Nancy Timely Tip

Your Active Prep is tackled immediately before the conversation. This pre-conversation prep is a discipline. Create space for a 5- or 15-minute routine to control your schedule and preserve the precious moments before you begin the conversation.

The remaining Actions for *Wait* direct our focus to this Active Prep to get your mind, eyes, and body ready to engage in the conversation. This starts with Action 3.

Active Prep Action 3: Eliminate Your Distractions

What are you doing immediately before your sales conversations? Are you trying to finish one more thing? Grab something to eat? Scramble to set up? These habits are dangerous. That's why *Waiting* starts with stopping. *Stopping* what? Everything else.

Take precautions to eliminate your distractions so you can be mentally present in your conversations, whether by phone, video, or in person. Turn off your cell phone and remove it from sight, turn off your computer screen, physically move away from your desk, or close your door. And, most importantly, no multitasking.

What? No multitasking? Yes—multitasking's detriments often outweigh the positives. Let's challenge the myth of multitasking. Many busy people believe that working on several things simultaneously—multitasking—makes them more efficient. This is why I often hear advisors brag about how good they are at multitasking and jokingly comment that it works well for them because they have an ADD personality. (However, I notice that I never hear *top* advisors saying this.)

Well, here's the deal: we do not *increase* our productivity by working on several things at the same time. Research by Dr. Edward Hallowell, a Massachusetts-based psychiatrist, whose book titled *CrazyBusy* remains the authority on the consequences of multitasking, found that multitasking efficiency is a myth. "It's the great seduction of the information age," he said in an interview on Cnet.com in 2008. "You can create the illusion of doing work and of being productive and creative when you're not. You're just treading water." Hallowell's research found that multitasking decreases productivity and gives us a false sense of what we are really accomplishing.

In an article published in the *Harvard Business Review* in January 2005, he describes a new condition that mimics ADD, called "attention deficit trait," which he says is "purely a response to the hyperkinetic environment in which we live." In other words, our desire to multitask is a response to the activity and rush around us.

"Never in history has the human brain been asked to track so many data points," writes Hallowell. Yet this challenge "can be controlled only by creatively engineering one's environment and one's emotional and physical health." Engineering your environment means reducing visual and audible distractions whenever possible. If you want to achieve the highest levels of productivity and success, you must stop believing that multitasking serves you well.

Need further proof? The amount of time lost in multitasking may surprise you. In 2005, researchers at the University of California, Irvine, found that when office workers were interrupted (phone calls, emails, Slack, or Teams channel messages) during a task, it took an average of 25 minutes to get back on task after the interruption. Yes, you read that correctly: 25 minutes of less effective efforts even after an interruption of just 2 or 3 minutes! Think of the number of interruptions we have in a day and do the math; that's a lot of lost time.

If you're thinking, "I would never get anything done if I only focused on one task at a time," you aren't alone. We are multitaskers by nature, and *some* multitasking is very effective for us. We *can* walk and talk at the same time. We can talk to a prospect and access our CRM system for information. We can eat and read the newspaper or our newsfeeds—and although I find that I can't remember what (or worse, how much) I ate, at least I am accomplishing two tasks at the same time.

That kind of multitasking is doable because one or both of the tasks do not require mental effort. It doesn't work when we try to multitask two mental-effort tasks. Our brains are unable to break from a mentally challenging task, such as working on a financial plan or a recommendation for a prospect or taking a phone call, and immediately return to the same level of focus and productivity. We lose something in the process—time, an idea, clarity. We then lose the opportunity to give the highest value to each task we are doing.

I have run into skeptics who challenge the research and argue that it doesn't take 25 minutes for them to refocus. When I hear this, I suggest they personally test the research. And Jason in Canada took the challenge. In his experiment, it took him over 7 hours to complete the straightforward task of inputting client information into his software. Constant distractions kept him from finishing the top item on his to-do list for nearly the entire workday.

Consider how multitasking affects your ability to focus on your prep and your prospect. When your mind attempts to focus on other tasks—different prospects, plans you need to complete, or a meeting with another client—your overall effectiveness is reduced.

How then do you break this cycle? By creating new habits that eliminate distractions before your sales conversations.

- Identify the common disruptions that keep you from preparing and focusing.
- Make a note of each time a disruption occurs for an entire day.
- Determine their importance in the context of your efforts—an interruption from your main prospect may be justified, less so those from standard emails or cell phone alerts.
- Develop a plan to eliminate these distractions (see my tips below).

Prioritize Each Morning

Address the most important items first, including your preparation for sales conversations. In his 2007 book titled *Eat that Frog*, best-selling author Brian Tracy wrote, "Mark Twain once said that if the first thing you do each morning is to eat a live frog, you can go through the day with the satisfaction of knowing that that is probably the *worst* thing that is going to happen to you all day long." In other words, complete the toughest task first each day to release the energy you would spend on avoiding or thinking about that task the rest of the day.

Schedule Time for Preparation

Schedule a specific block of time each day or week on your calendar for preparation. Then carefully preserve this time block.

Minimize the Inflow

Reduce the number of times your messages, or notifications, are loaded on all your electronics. Although most apps and software settings load your messages every 3 to 5 minutes, you can change this. Many email programs allow you to limit the number of times your emails are loaded in a day. And you can mute your internal chat programs as well, if needed.

Put Down Your Smartphone

Your smartphone's immediate access to email and updates on social media has created a false sense of urgency. Research shows that having your phone in sight distracts your brain as it constantly monitors it. Move your phone out of sight if possible.

Take Care of Basic Needs

Prepare to take care of basic human needs for yourself and for your prospect so your brain can be more present and focused during the conversation. Prepare a drink for you and, if you're meeting in person, for your prospects. Use the restroom before the meeting. A full bladder has been found to be as distracting as having a .05 blood alcohol level![5]

Ask for Time to Finish

Don't you hate it when you are deeply focused and someone interrupts you? Most of us will stop whatever we are doing and focus on that interruption. Instead, ask permission to finish your thought or action or to make a note. Say something like, "Hello, good to hear from you. Can you give me 2 minutes to finish the sentence I was typing so I can then focus on you?" Of course, you should adapt that message to your Tribal Type and situation. Most people will oblige, and if they don't, then you know it is urgent (if only in their minds).

Though no one can schedule and control every distraction, we have more control over our multitasking than we think. After all, if you don't respond to someone's email in the next 3 minutes, nothing earth-shattering will happen. Resisting that distraction should make you more productive with the time you otherwise would have lost.

Once you have eliminated distractions immediately before the conversation, it's time for a last review of notes!

---

5   MS Lewis et al, "The Effect of Acute Increase in Urge to Void on Cognitive Function in Healthy Adults," Neurourol Urodyn, 30, no.1 (January 2011): 183–7, https://doi: 10.1002/nau.20963.

CHAPTER 18

Wait Step: Final Active Prep Actions

Block time, protect that time, and use that time to break
your preoccupation and ready yourself to focus on WiifT.

—A Nancy Timely Tip

The final 2 Actions for the *Wait* step provide instructions for your final moments and minutes of pre-conversation.

Blocking time, protecting that time, and using that time to break your preoccupation and ready yourself to focus on WiifT will allow you to help your prospect break their own preoccupation when the conversation begins.

Active Prep Action 4: Review Notes Prior to Conversation

Immediately before the conversation, review the Quick Prep Tool and any other notes you have on the prospect and situation to refresh yourself on what is most important, how you will begin the conversation, and the decision you'll seek at the end of the conversation. This may only take a few minutes.

Action 5: Prepare Your Mind to Engage with the Prospect

The first 3 Actions for *Wait* are tangible and visual. Your hands or eyes are "on" something, whether it's the QPT, your clothes, or your environment. However, you also must prepare your mind.

Consider these situations: Your phone rings; you arrive at the prospect's location; you are sitting at your desk, waiting for the prospects to arrive; you start to make a call—what are you thinking about at that moment? Are you focusing on your prospects and the value you may bring to Them? Or are you thinking about some other situation?

Of course, your focus should be on the prospect or client. Renee Schuster of Rockwood Wealth Management has come up with an ingenious way to help her team focus on WiifT. She has a rule that other clients and situations can't be discussed as her team assembles in the conference room before a prospect or client arrives. It's all about who is coming in next!

Winning conversations—and conversions—begin in your head. Top performers in any discipline often cite mental preparation as critical to their success.

Baseball Hall of Fame player Hank Aaron (who played for my home team, the Milwaukee Brewers) attributed much of his success to his mental preparation—before and during the game. He believed that mental preparation and doing his homework were integral to becoming a great, consistent hitter year after year.

Aaron was an athlete before many of you were born. Yet his message of preparation and homework still holds true today for world-class athletes and sellers. I've heard many top-performing salespeople say they are more successful when they are in the right frame of mind before any sales call.

This pause for mental preparation is the final Action for the *Wait* step because it is the last thing you should do immediately before contact with a prospect. No matter how you connect with your prospects—telephone, video, email, or a face-to-face visit—your final Action should be preparing your mind to engage with them. *Waiting* and "getting your head in the game" saves both you and your prospect time during your conversations.

Follow these tips for your mental preparation:

Visualize Your Success

Some athletes and artists visualize every part of their upcoming competition or performance, including the outcome. Mentally work through the conversation, then focus on visualizing a positive outcome—for you and the prospect.

Develop a Routine

Your routine is a repeatable process, a series of habits you develop to prepare yourself. Determine 2 actions for your mental prep, then pause and do them before your conversation.

After observing other people's success with mental preparation, I created a routine before my training workshops. Instead of making final phone calls, I spend a few minutes thinking and sometimes repeating out loud, "It's not about me, it's about them." It keeps my ego intact and focused on the people with whom I am about to engage.

Use Positive Self-talk

Tell yourself that the conversation will be productive and value-filled for all involved. Prospects can "hear" your self-talk and beliefs through your tone and word choice. I once received a message on my business line from a salesperson who said things like, "A callback will probably not happen, but I'm trying," and "You can look at our website before calling me, but that's wishful thinking."

What do you think this salesperson's mental prep and self-talk were like before calling me? Dread? Fear? Wishful thinking? It's doubtful their thoughts were positive or focused on success. Now, if their strategy was to make me feel bad for them, it almost worked! This is a good example of the confidence discussed in Chapter 1. The salesperson needed to build their confidence before picking up the phone. They definitely were not able to fake it.

Ditch Your Pitch to Keep Your Prospect from Ducking Your Efforts

If you want to have collaborative conversations with prospective clients consider how your mindset and language about selling impact your prospect's reaction.

Some people unknowingly create unnecessary barriers between them and their prospects through their language use. For instance, consider the word "pitch." You may hear statements like these:

- "I'm looking to get better at my pitch."
- "My pitch really worked."
- "I'm working on my sales pitch materials."

I also know of teams who have a Pitch Book. While I understand the intention of the term "pitch" in sales, its use and connotation often confuse me. In a collaborative selling approach focused on WiifT, how does "pitching to someone" fit? Think about it. If you are being pitched to, what are your options? You can bat it away, let it hit you, or duck.

This is not how I want my prospect to respond in a conversation. How about you? And how do you think a prospect likes being "pitched to"? These types of old-school sales terms may make prospects feel like they are being manipulated. Instead, we can keep our prospects from ducking or batting away our solution by preparing our minds to engage with prospects professionally and collaboratively as we focus on WiifT.

I beg you: please ditch the pitch in your vocabulary and mind!

This mental preparation is truly the start of working with your prospects in a genuine, WiifT-focused, and value-filled way.

* * * * *

Your collaborative sales conversation begins with a WiifT attitude as you review your notes, your QPT, and any other research you have completed. This *Wait* step allows you to stop, break your own preoccupation, prepare, and engage your mind so you can focus on them.

CHAPTER 19

Quick Tips and Best Practices for Preparing for Your Sales Conversation

As you implement the *Wait* step, use these *Wait*-related quick tips and best practices, from advisors who have completed the Genuine Sales 12-week course. There's also a success story to show the concepts in action.

Quick Tips for the Wait Step of WIIFT

- Make the time to prepare on paper or screen. Use the Quick Prep Tool™ to identify the conversation objective and outline the entire conversation from start to finish.

- Create specific Quick Prep Tool templates for each step in your sales process. Populate it with the most common questions you ask and information you share. Then personalize it for each situation as it arises.

- Research the person, couple, or family to ensure your conversation will be relevant and value-focused throughout.

🔥 Adjust the information and materials for the prospect's Tribal Type.

🔥 Look in the mirror to ensure your personal presentation is favorable.

🔥 Gather any materials you may need and ensure they represent you and your company positively.

🔥 Eliminate potential distractions before you enter the room, start the videoconference, or pick up the phone.

🔥 Mentally prepare to engage with your prospect before picking up the phone or walking through the door.

Advisor's Best Practices and Tips for Preparation

🔥 Turn off notifications and email 10 minutes before the meeting.

🔥 Take a walk, stretch, or exercise 10 minutes before the meeting.

🔥 Do 1 or 2 minutes of deep breathing and/or positive talk immediately before the meeting.

🔥 Close all unnecessary windows and programs—no multitasking.

🔥 Set up relevant materials for screen sharing. Close or move other things to another screen.

🔥 Have visuals or handouts available for meetings—create a few different versions based on Tribal Types.

🔥 Practice the 3-Step Start. (Explained in Chapter 20)

🔥 Plan to help Them break their preoccupation.

🔥 Imagine and plan the first part of the conversation.

🔥 Think of the meeting outcome as a collaboratively happy place. Visualize a positive outcome.

🐚 Put your phone face down.

🐚 Every conversation is with a different person in a different situation, so take a breath and reevaluate before starting.

🐚 Review questions before meetings to ensure they're open-ended and queue a list of follow-up questions.

Success!

Chuck, from New York, had a prospect stall in the sales process. She was always pleasant, but she would not make a decision. Chuck stepped back to think about what he knew about her Tribal Type and how the approach he had been using may have affected the stalled decision.

To prepare for the next conversation, we researched the prospect online, looking at her social pages and company website to see if we could find clues of what she needed to make the decision. We found information on the company website that explained what was important to her: her family and people in general.

With that information, Chuck realized that she needed to feel more connected to him. He prepared connection questions and feedback questions that focused on emotions and her family.

In the next conversation, he used his preparation notes and shared more personal interest and asked the question he created about the impact of the decision on those she cared most about.

That was it! She officially became a client that day.

–CHUCK, NY

CHAPTER 20

Initiate: Win Them at Hello with a Purposeful Start

"Be brave enough to start
a conversation that matters."

—Dau Voire

"Client experience" has been a buzz phrase for years. And that experience is created from the first millisecond of your conversation. These are the first moments that determine much of the value for the rest of your conversation.

After the *Wait* step, you are ready to connect with your prospect—the actual start of the two-way conversation. Yet quickly moving into a sales pitch or agenda item can create a "hold on!" reaction from the prospect that ends the conversation before it really gets started. Instead, engage the prospect in a collaborative conversation focused on Them—with a purposeful start.

The *Initiate* step of WIIFT opens the door to a value-filled conversation, sets expectations, and most importantly, connects you with the person(s) in the conversation with you. Doing this builds trust, breaks their preoccupation with other matters, and earns you the right to have the two-way information exchange needed for a collaborative conversation. Purposefully *Initiating* your conversation ensures that *this* conversation will be productive for all of you.

Consider this: though you are prepared for the conversation, the prospect may not be. I don't know of any prospect who sits around with pen in hand waiting for you, even for a scheduled appointment. Do you?

For most situations, you can expect that the prospect is preoccupied, doing or thinking of something else, until the moment you connect. *Initiating* is important for both of you, and preparation keeps you from wasting time—yours and theirs.

The Initiate Step Overview

 ### Objectives

✓ Connect with them before business begins
✓ Build trust
✓ Break preoccupation
✓ Earn the right to ask questions

 ### Actions/How-tos

1. Greet
2. Explain why you are connecting
3. Ask questions to engage them and get them talking
4. Use appropriate eye contact and open ears
5. Focus on what they are communicating—both words and intent

Though there is considerable flexibility in how you Initiate the conversation, there is a method to the madness of starting the conversation.

The Anchor to Initiate

How much time do you have to engage your prospect? While it varies, their first impression of you affects the level and speed of the engagement. And this impression is formed quickly. When you are face-to-face, first impressions are formed by your overall approach, including how you look, whether your face is smiling or stern, and the items you have with you.

Research by Janine Willis and Alexander Todorov of Princeton University in 2005 found that first impressions are made in between 100 and 500 milliseconds.[6] They discovered that it only takes a tenth of a second to form an impression of a stranger from their face and that longer exposures don't significantly alter those impressions, although longer exposure might boost confidence in their initial judgments.

100 milliseconds is literally the blink of an eye. This is why I place so much emphasis on preparation. You must be ready and focused to help them get ready and focus!

Then you must consciously and consistently start your conversation. The anchor to the *Initiate* step forms the first 3 Actions, called the 3-Step Start.

3-Step Start™

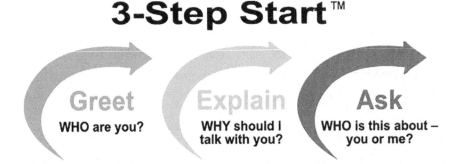

Greet	Explain	Ask
WHO are you?	**WHY should I talk with you?**	**WHO is this about – you or me?**

---

[6] Janine Willis and Alexander Todorov, "First Impressions: Making up Your Mind after a 100-MS Exposure to a Face," *Psychological Science* 17, no.7 (July 2006): 592–98, http://www.jstor.org/stable/40064417.

The 3-Step Start

The start of your conversation is not just about you. It's about you *and* Them!

The first 3 Actions of the *Initiate* step—the 3-Step Start—are your anchor and guide to what you say or write to start the conversation. These Actions, which can be adapted to *Initiate* any conversation, connect you to Them quickly.

And you need that immediate connection, as your prospect is most likely distracted and may still be wondering whether they should talk with you or not. Emotions are likely at play. The prospect may be nervous, excited, anxious, hopeful, fearful, or a combination of these. And when they first hear you or see you, they may have these unstated questions in mind:

- Who are you? Are you credible? Can I trust you?
- Why are we talking or taking time for this?
- Is this worth my time? Am I in the right place?
- Who is this really about? Do you want to pitch something at me or to help me?

Your ability to answer these unstated questions quickly breaks their preoccupation and sets the stage for a collaborative and engaged conversation. The prospect's unspoken questions need to be addressed efficiently and purposefully *every* time because connecting Them to *each* conversation earns you the right to proceed.

The 3-Step Start answers the prospect's unstated questions. For example:

"Good afternoon, Zeenath, I am Luis Ortiz with Finessed Financial. We scheduled this time to discuss your questions about your retirement readiness. Does this time still work for you? *(Pause for response.)* No? Can we reschedule for tomorrow morning at 9 a.m.?"

"Good morning, Carol, I am Ramesh Jafar with Atlantic Wealth Management. How are you today? Am I calling at the time you expected? *(Pause for response.)* Great! You thought you would have about 90 minutes to discuss your finances postdivorce. Does that still work for you?"

"Hello and thank you for inviting me to talk with your group today. I am Mike Haubrich of Financial Service Group. We partner with our clients through life's transitions to keep their financial peace of mind. During our 60 minutes together today, we will share with you 3 important items that you need to know to ensure your investments are safe for your financial well-being. Let's start with introductions. Would you please share your name and tell us what's the best financial decision you've ever made?"

Although the primary focus in this chapter is on the scheduled conversation, you can also adjust the 3-Step Start for cold outreach (yes, some advisors still do this effectively), written communication, client meetings, and your team meetings.

You will adapt and adjust the 3-Step Start for your own personal, value-filled conversation starter depending upon:

- Your relationship with the prospect

- The objective of the conversation

- The prospect's Tribal Type

- The mode of contact—face-to-face, video, phone, or written

- The number of people involved

- Whether you are initiating the conversation or on the receiving end of an inbound contact

Now that you've been introduced to the *Initiate* step's 3-Step Start, the next chapter provides the how-tos for each component of this flexible framework. And the final 2 Actions of *Initiate*, covered in Chapter 22, will illuminate the nuances that guarantee effective communication from the beginning of your conversation until the end.

CHAPTER 21

Initiate: The 3-Step Start How-tos

*It's not small talk at all.
Connection is about "smart talk."*

—A Nancy Timely Tip

Many interesting human dynamics affect the first minutes of a conversation. That's why the *Initiate* step is so important, so that *your* dynamics aren't a barrier. This chapter will share the 3-Step Start's how-tos as well as important tidbits about the whys behind the how-tos.

Action 1: Greet

In the 3-Step Start, Greet is the first Action. Clearly introduce yourself with these specifics:

A salutation. Begin your conversations with a positive, sincere greeting. For example: "Hello," "Good morning/afternoon," "Great to see you," or "Hola!" Address them by name when possible. For new prospects, use their proper names. Don't shorten someone's name unless they have given you permission.

Your name. Adapt this for your prospect's familiarity with you, your personal style, and your comfort level. Some advisors just use their first name, while others always use both their first and last names. Your company may have a preference. State your name clearly and add an interesting connection if possible. For instance, if your name was Joann Sleight, you could say your name and then make it memorable by saying "Sleight, like Santa's sleigh with a T added." If you have an unusual or hard-to-pronounce first or last name, you could use it as a conversation opener.

Company name. Identify your company by name and any other specific differentiators, like location, if needed. Prospects don't want to rack their brain trying to make the connection.

Adjust your greeting to your Tribe, the situation, and the prospect. Don't assume they know or remember you or your company.

Make the First Moments Count

The first words you and your prospects say to each other set the tone for the rest of the conversation. This short Action is often rushed through as mere "words" instead of an opportunity to answer one of the unstated questions prospects have upon contact: "Who are you?"

Purposeful first moments are invaluable in every conversation. They demonstrate you are prepared, organized, focused on them, and, most importantly, that you won't waste their time. A sincere greeting immediately connects them to you as a person and sparks engagement.

After you Greet your prospects and introduce yourself, *pause* to allow them to reciprocate. The sooner they begin talking, the faster you set the stage for a two-way information exchange.

The formality of introducing yourself varies widely depending on the situation and style. This is *not* the time to give your "speech" or to talk about what you do.

Once the Greeting is over, you will move between the next two steps in the 3-Step Start more fluidly according to the flow of conversation.

Explain

WHY should I talk with you?

Action 2: Explain Why You Are Connecting

To set expectations and quickly address unstated questions like "What are we doing?" "Will we talk about what I want to?" and "Is this worth my time?" explain the meeting agenda and objective. Then collaborate by asking if they'd like to clarify anything. What they share will allow you to confirm, collect information, or adjust your approach. If they ask to add an action or topic that will not be relevant in this conversation, you can set the proper expectation that this should be part of a different conversation. (Ahem, I'm hoping to get some advice today on which options to choose for my 401k enrollment.)

Your explanation may also include specifics on what their role or decision will be today. For example, you can say, "You will not be asked to make a final decision today. Your only decision is whether you want to take the next step in the process," or "After today's conversation, you'll have all you need to make a decision."

This is an important time to avoid using minimizer words in the conversation. Steer clear of sentences like "We're *just* meeting to _____," "We're *just* going to talk *a little* about your goals today," and "I'll share a *little* information about how we work with people like you." Watch for more on minimizing wimpy words in later chapters!

Fill Your Introduction with Value

New prospects may need more than just an introduction. They need Proof—the umbrella over WIIFT®—to justify and validate why they should talk with you.

This *value statement* is a proof point for who you are, what this is about, and What's in it for Them. When stating why you are contacting the prospect, connect the reason to a WiifT or include an appropriate value statement.

Action 3: Ask Questions to Get Them Talking

An easy way to turn the focus to Them and get them talking as early as possible is to ask questions. In the *Initiate* step, you'll use two kinds of questions—Time and Connection.

Time to Talk?

Show that you value their time by addressing it very early in the conversation. Define the amount of time you expect to take or confirm the time already scheduled. By addressing time, you can determine the pace of the conversation, reschedule if necessary, and alleviate any fears or concerns they have about time. Here are some examples of what to say:

"We have 30 minutes scheduled. Does that sound okay?"

"So that we make good use of our time, how much time did you plan for our conversation?"

"Does this time still work for you?"

"We have 45 minutes scheduled for this conversation. In order to monitor our time best, do you have a hard stop?"

Their response to the time question tells you if you can move forward as planned or if you need to adjust the agenda or reschedule to a more convenient time. Whether your conversation is scheduled or not, clarifying time allows many people to stop focusing on time, because they know *you* are. It demonstrates that you are considerate, paying attention to time, and not going to waste *their* time. I strongly believe addressing time shows respect and demonstrates your desire to collaborate and make it about *Them*.

Time questions and Tribal Type

🖎 Achievers always have time on their mind. Confirming or asking about it reassures Them that you will keep things moving. Often they will say, "We have 60 minutes scheduled, but I hope we can finish in 40 so I can get to my next meeting." You'll know it's a valuable conversation when they stop looking at their watch, phone, or surroundings.

🖎 Commanders want to control the time and tell you how much time is needed or available. They will also expect that you stick to whatever time they set. Pay close attention to time and check in throughout the conversation.

🪝 Reflectors need to know they will have time to have a complete conversation, get information, and have their questions answered. Their concern is whether you are going to rush them. By confirming and clarifying the amount of time you have planned, you reduce this concern.

🪝 Expressers may not think of time. They are flexible and generous with the time they will give you. Your job is to keep the conversation on track to accomplish your shared objective.

Turn the Focus to Them with Connection Questions

The second type of question turns the focus to them specifically: Connection questions. Yup, the dreaded "small talk" so many of you worry about. But really it is "smart talk." Connection questions *Initiate* the conversation. The prospect's responses provide insight and a connection for you to build from.

Please note Connection questions often flow naturally after exchanging greetings. Connection and Time questions do not have to be asked together.

Connection questions provide opportunities to engage the person and *connect* with Them. These questions are about Them, not your solution or agenda, and could be about anything from the weather or a common point in your background to their family, their interest in sports, or their relationship or career.

Asking connection questions—and hearing their response—is your opportunity to break their preoccupation, observe Tribal Type clues and their level of openness to you, and find out more about them.

While some prospects may push to move directly to the agenda after confirming time, don't assume all will, even if that's your personal preference. Many willing prospects *want* to connect with you personally first. You may be surprised at how many prospects will engage with you when given the opportunity to do so, especially if they are asked a question they want to answer! However, if they give a short, curt response to a connection question, don't push it. Instead, move forward to the *Investigate* step.

Ideas for Connection questions

- An occasion they recently experienced on their own or with you
- The time of year
- Current events
- Who they are associated with
- Past experiences
- Other interests
- Their career
- The status of something you both know about
- Work projects, family events, hobbies, vacations
- A work transition
- Topics from past conversations

How you prefer to start a sales conversation doesn't matter as much as how *They* prefer to begin and what *They* want to talk about. So plan your connection questions to be relevant to Them by:

- Reviewing notes from previous conversations or your online research
- Asking others who know the person or situation to identify the most probable and relevant questions
- Using the details a prospect shares or their environment

For example, an advisor noticed a trophy on a shelf behind the prospect during a virtual conversation. Their discussion about the trophy, a coveted cultural award from her former job, consumed 70% of their time together and led to scheduling the next appointment before the meeting ended. The advisor told me the second meeting ended in an easy conversion.

Connection questions for each Tribal Type

Knowing a prospect's Tribal Type can guide you to the right question to ask. Depending on the Tribe, asking about the weather, their family, or their weekend plans might work—or should be avoided!

Achievers and Commanders often respond better to fact or situation-based connection questions rather than personal ones.

- "Last time we spoke, you mentioned that _____. How's that going?"
- "How is _____ working out?"
- "What did you think of _____ (insert an event, relevant news, our last meeting)?"
- "How long have you been interested in (or searched for) _____ (insert topic)?"

Reflectors and Expressers, on the other hand, will respond favorably to personal questions. Ask about themselves, others they know, or how they feel about something in the news, the weather, their family, or their company. For example:

- "Jim Smith, who introduced us, said he used to work with you. How long did you work together?"
- "How was your weekend?"
- "I see that your phone number has an Arizona area code. How long have you lived there?"

- ✍ "You mentioned in your LinkedIn profile that you graduated from the University of Toronto. What led you to attend that college?"

- ✍ "How do you feel about _____ (insert an event, relevant news, your last meeting)?"

- ✍ "What do you like or dislike about _____ (insert their job or location)?"

TIMELY TIP

Discussing religion or politics is frequently a conversation-stopper. Criticizing or complaining about others, including your competition, can also shut down a conversation quickly—you never know the prospect's connection to your competition! Possibly the biggest conversation stopper is you doing most or all of the talking. Give them the opportunity to talk as soon as possible.

The Pause Time

Pause Time, also known as "response latency," is the amount of time you pause after asking a question of someone else. It's the interval during which the person allows the other party to process the question and formulate an answer.

Most people only wait between 1 and 3 seconds before asking another question, repeating the question, or moving on. I know I've been guilty of this! Many years ago, a Reflector shared with me that when I ask a question and then try to rush her through an answer, it frustrates her and shuts down her thought process. This closes any opportunity for her to meaningfully contribute ideas and solutions. She reminded me that I need to pause, especially if I've asked a thought-provoking or detailed question, and wait for the response.

I've observed that some people, when asked to recall information or share reflections, may need between 8 and 20 seconds to formulate their response mentally *and* then begin to verbalize that response. That's a *long* time to remain quiet and stay focused without multi-tasking, answering the question yourself, or beginning to ask other questions. However, the pause is usually well worth the discomfort of being silent for a short time.

For telephone conversations, however, a shorter pause of 6 to 8 seconds is most effective. Longer than that makes the prospect wonder if you hung up on them.

3-Step Starts with Inbound and Outbound Calls

Outbound 3-Step Starts for prospects with whom you have had previous contact are the same as with face-to-face conversations you *Initiate*. Incoming phone conversations, on the other hand, give you an advantage because the person calling has proactively contacted you, presumably *wanting* to talk with you. The objective of *Initiating* the conversation from your end remains the same: connect with the prospect to build trust, engage them to break their preoccupation with other matters, and earn the right to ask questions to clarify and discover how you or your solution can address the POWNs they called about.

Though the prospect is calling you, your purposeful initiation allows you to take control and be more than a reactive order-taker. You can quickly set the stage to be *in* the conversation with them and earn the right to expand the conversation to discover POWNs that increase your sales probability and opportunity.

With minor adjustments, the 3-Step Start is effective when *Initiating* telephone inbound calls:

1. **Greet** with a welcoming salutation, identifying your company and your name.

2. **Explain** that you appreciate their call.

3. **Ask** for their name when possible and how you can assist them.

Use these 3 elements in the order and flow that fits your situation:

"Good morning and thank you for calling Express Financial. This is Karla. How may I assist you?"

"Hello, I appreciate you reaching out to Smiley Wealth Management. This is Kevin. What can I help you with today?"

"Greetings. This is Jackson with the Financial Futures Firm. Thank you for calling. May I have your name?"

Add value to inbound sales opportunities by focusing on the person on the other end of the call. Create a genuine connection with the prospect, assess how they want to communicate with you at that moment, and move forward to earn the right to open the sales opportunity.

Written Conversation Starts

Written correspondence allows you time to make the 3-Step Start just right. This pays off because you have a very short time to grab their attention before they press the delete key, toss the letter in the trash, or add the message to their long to-do list to address later!

Your written 3-Step Start should include:

Greet with a salutation that includes their name, so it doesn't look like a form message.

Explain specifically why you are writing. This should include your introduction and any connection you have to them if they don't know you.

Ask for their attention or the request for action sooner rather than later.

Make a positive start, whether it is an email or a physical letter:

- Use a relevant subject line.
- Present a clear, concise, and logical message.
- Clearly request or state the action you desire—the reason for the connection.

- Give them the option to respond to you by email, postal letter, text, or telephone. Include all your contact information. (You might be surprised who will pick up the phone and call you!)

- End with a personalized salutation and your name.

* * * * *

The *Initiate* step is your first opportunity to engage the prospect and begin learning about Them and what is important to Them. See? It's not small talk at all. Connection is about "smart talk."

When you *Initiate* your conversations, be sure to adapt the 3-Step Start to the situation. You may find that sometimes using all 3 steps in quick succession for outbound, unplanned cold prospects works well. For most conversations, though, this is a joint effort. You greet, pause to listen to their response, and return their greeting. Then you explain or remind them why you are connecting, let them contribute their thoughts to the objective and agenda, and then ask a question to engage Them.

There you have it: the introduction to the 3-Step Start. This anchor allows you to consistently *Initiate* the conversation, no matter the objective.

CHAPTER 22

Initiate: The Nuances of Initiate

The ultimate objective of Initiate is to earn the right to move forward collaboratively in the conversation.

—A Nancy Timely Tip

Successful *Initiations* are more than *what* you say in the 3-Step Start. *How* you fully communicate and "show up" at the beginning of your conversation is just as important. You need to listen, make eye contact, and focus on Them to engage and connect with the prospect.

These are parts of the necessary professional presence, or as leadership expert Sylvia Ann Hewlett defines it, "a combination of gravitas, communication, and appearance." These are the nuances of *Initiating* your conversation.

Action 4: Use Appropriate Eye Contact and Open Ears

You'll connect more fully with the prospect when you incorporate your eyes and ears from the first moment of contact.

Make Appropriate Eye Contact

Making eye contact is an old but classic communication tip. Your eyes are a powerful tool to make a deeper connection and ensure you are clearly communicating your message.

What you do with your eyes sends a message about what is important to you. Your eyes are beams that illuminate what you are focused on, even with virtual conversations. When you focus on Them, you demonstrate that you are paying attention and that they matter.

While eye contact is essential for connecting in face-to-face and video conversations, the question, "How much eye contact should I make?" is tough to answer! There isn't an easy formula for making the right amount of eye contact, but using *appropriate* eye contact is the key.

Appropriate eye contact is achieved when you pay attention to the prospect's signals to determine what is comfortable for them. I've had conversations where I had a hard time looking down to take notes because of the prospect's intense eye contact. Some people are *not* comfortable with direct eye contact, while others will stop talking if you look away. A person's comfort level often depends on their confidence or Tribal Type, but it may also depend on their gender or cultural background. You'll need to find the right amount of eye contact for each situation by paying attention.

This is also true in virtual/video conversations. My dear friend Julie Hansen, an expert in video communications and author of *Look Me in the Eye*, recommends 2 specific actions for using your eyes during a virtual sales conversation.

🪙 *"Look 'em in the eyes."* Strive to keep your eyes on the camera lens at least two-thirds of the time when building a relationship.

🪙 *Use your peripheral vision.* Use peripheral vision to read major changes in your prospect's body language or expression.

Appropriate eye contact allows you to see their reaction as you *Initiate* your conversation, allowing you to adjust quickly to make the prospect comfortable. Matching eye contact with open ears makes this easier.

Listen with Open Ears

You may find yourself talking too much in prospect conversations for all sorts of reasons, causing you to focus more on *telling* than collaboratively *selling*. Though you need to be yourself while positioning who you are and why they should talk to you, you can also quickly talk yourself out of a sales opportunity if you're not careful. Most prospects will shut you out or close the conversation if they think you are wasting their time by talking *at* them.

Use open ears to make ear contact and keep the conversation open. When you ask a question, they need you to do more than just wait to talk. You need to pause and listen for the response. I describe this kind of effective, active listening as "ear contact." Your ears can be used very effectively to connect to their words, intent, and emotion and to notice the hot buttons that may make or break your sale. Ear contact is especially important in situations without a visual connection, such as phone or text conversations.

If you need further proof of the importance of listening, research from Gong found that in conversations with prospects, top-performing sellers spend 46% of the time talking and 54% of the time listening while bottom-performing sellers spent 72% of the time talking and only 28% of the time listening.

To make good ear contact, use open ears both in the *Initiate* step and throughout the whole conversation with these tips:

- *Listen without distractions.* Stop multitasking!

- *Take notes on key points to help you focus on this conversation.* Even if you use AI to capture notes, make some physical notes if it helps you focus. Then refer to these notes in your preparation for future conversations.

- *Postpone evaluating what they are saying and just listen.* Don't start mentally composing your answer while they're still talking.

- *Paraphrase the information they share.* You will listen more carefully when you know you need to paraphrase the information.

Using open ears allows you to "hear" opportunities that you can then translate into sales.

Action 5: Focus on What They Are Communicating — Words and Intent

The last Action for the *Initiate* step is to focus on what They are communicating—words and intent. This builds on key aspects of the *Wait* step—eliminate distractions and multitasking in order to be present in *this* conversation with *this* person at *this* time—and on Action 4 (appropriate eye contact and open ears).

Along with those visual cues, you also want to focus on their emotions, motives, and energy associated with their words. They are sending you signals about what is important to Them.

Your eyes are important throughout the conversation for more than direct eye contact. Observe everything about their movements and environment.

You will get key information about their real message when you pay attention "in the moment." Notice their pace and body language;

be aware of hesitations, nervousness, and confidence. These valuable unspoken messages let you gauge the probability of the sales opportunity, allowing you to spend your time on the most probable opportunities in your pipeline.

I recently observed a sales conversation recorded through Zoom with an advisor and her prospective clients, a husband and wife with no children. Because I wasn't emotionally connected to the conversation, I could objectively observe the prospects' body language.

When the advisor started discussing 529 plans for this couple's future children, their body language showed discomfort and impatience. They made side-eyes to each other. One moved their chair, and they both started looking away.

Their body language clearly showed this was not a topic they cared about. The advisor never noticed.

Earn the Right to Move Forward in the Conversation

All the Actions of *Initiate* lead you to the ultimate objective: to *earn the right to move forward collaboratively* in the conversation. When you focus on engaging and connecting with them (as opposed to going into a pitch), the prospect is more willing to discuss their POWNs. They will give you permission to move into the *Investigate* step and provide the information that qualifies them and the potential opportunity. Your preparation makes all those things easier.

So, how do you earn the right to move forward? By:

- Connecting with the prospect
- Showing that you are listening to them
- Respecting their time limits
- Understanding the customs of their particular Tribe

Your preparation makes all of those things easier.

After listening to their responses to connection questions, it is easy to segue into the *Investigation* with a comment such as, "It is good to hear that you enjoy your job. Are you ready to move to the specific questions I have for you today?" or "I understand you are pressed for time, let's get to the reason we're talking."

The subtle feel of the way you approach the conversation differentiates you from the competition and sets you up to collaboratively *Investigate* the prospects' POWNs productively. When they have let you in and engaged in the conversation with you, it's a good start to collaboration.

Adjust Your Initiation to the Situation

So far, I've mainly focused on face-to-face conversations with one prospect. With a few adjustments, you can use the 3-Step Start to *Initiate* telephone, written, and couple or group sales conversations.

Tips for Telephone Conversations

First impressions on the telephone are created from the first words you say, the tone of your voice, and background noises. One easy way to make a favorable impression in telephone conversations is to smile.

Have you ever heard that people can hear you smile? It's true! A 2008 study through the University of Portsmouth in England found that smiles could be discerned without visual cues.[7] Pablo Arias, PhD student in cognitive science at IRCAM in Paris, calls it "auditory smiling." The research found that not only could callers identify if the telephone speaker was smiling, but they were also able to determine the *type* of smile.

---

[7] Emmanuel Ponsot, Pablo Arias, and Jean-Julien Aucouturier, "Uncovering Mental Representations of Smiled Speech Using Reverse Correlation," Journal of the Acoustical Society of America 143, no.1 (January 2018): EL19– EL24.

Did you know there are different types of smiles? I didn't, but the study participants were able to discern a Duchenne smile, which is a full smile involving the crinkling of the eyes, from a non-Duchenne smile, where the eyes are not involved. A Duchenne smile is considered a more natural and genuine smile. This research is proof that the smile in your voice *is* heard by the person on the other end.

Additional ways to make a positive first impression over the telephone include:

- Keep the tone and pitch of your voice steady, upbeat, and energetic
- Minimize or eliminate interruptions
- Use audibles
- Verbalize what you are doing throughout the conversation

Minimize unnecessary noises. Callers hear when you shuffle papers, click a pen, or type on a keyboard. As I conducted phone interviews with advisor candidates looking to join client firms, I could hear candidates turn water on and off, eat, open and close doors, and more.

Verbalize what you're doing. If you enter information using the keyboard, tell the prospect what you are doing so they don't wonder about it; for example: "You will hear me clicking on the keyboard as I look up that information for you" or, "I'm making a note of what you are telling me."

Initiating to a Couple or Group

If you have two or more prospects in one conversation, adjust the 3-Step Start to engage the whole "gang."

Multiple people present additional dynamics that impact your conversations. For example, some people will act differently in the group setting than they did in a one-on-one conversation. I'm sure you've noticed that with couples.

When working with one couple, an advisor observed that the wife exhibited an Achiever personality when she wasn't with her husband. She conversed in a quick, time-constrained way. Yet with the husband present, she became talkative, friendly, and eager to ensure that her husband got to share his thoughts throughout the entire conversation.

To make *Initiations* successful with multiple people, don't assume that each person knows who you are, why you are meeting with them, why they are there, or the objective of the conversation. Use the 3-Step Start to focus on everyone present, engage Them, and move the conversation forward:

✄ **Greet** by using a salutation, name, and company name.

✄ **Explain** why the group is talking or meeting.

- Use a summary statement or PowerPoint slide to focus on why you are meeting.

- Acknowledge who you have met/talked with prior to the meeting.

- Prepare a value statement that connects with different Tribal Types. If telling a story or testimonial, use names and metrics and be sure to include supporting proof.

- Clarify the time scheduled for the meeting and provide an agenda or overview of what will be covered.

✄ **Ask** questions to engage each person. Ask each person to answer a question, such as "What do you want to ensure we cover today?" or "What can we do to make this a good use of your time?"

- Your purposeful and prepared *Initiation* allows you to capture the attention of all those in the party and help all of Them focus on the same topic.

CHAPTER 23

Quick Tips and Best Practices for Initiating a Collaborative Conversation

As you implement the *Initiate* step, use these quick tips and best practices, from advisors who have completed the Genuine Sales 12-week course. There's also a success story to show the concepts in action.

Quick Tips

- Consistently use the 3-Step Start—Greet, Explain, and Ask—to begin your conversations.

- Adjust the order, formality, and language of the Start to the specific situation and Tribal Type.

- Prepare and practice how you will begin a conversation, especially for new buyer situations.

- In couple or group situations, ask a connection question that allows each person the opportunity to engage if they so choose.

- Clearly state your objective and connect it to a WiifT.

🖋 When prospects say they have time but hurry up, or that they have just a minute, use the little time you have with them to reschedule a better time.

🖋 Pause after you ask a question. Rushing will not make them want to talk more. Focus on waiting 10 to 15 seconds when face-to-face and 6 to 8 seconds on the phone.

🖋 Smile whether you're meeting face-to-face or on the telephone. Let them see and hear that you are welcoming and glad to be talking with them.

🖋 Maintain eye contact and practice open ears.

🖋 Be on time, confident, and positive.

🖋 Look for unspoken messages in their body language to discern their intent, emotions, and motivations.

Advisor's Best Practices and Tips for Initiating Conversations

🖋 Develop an awareness of Initiate as a step.

🖋 Reference the QPT. It includes the Initiate step, among other good things not to forget.

🖋 Make a great first impression by being friendly and using good eye contact.

🖋 Be fully focused.

🖋 Stay curious.

🖋 Be ready to slow down, engage, and break their preoccupation.

🖋 Set the tone for the rest of the conversation.

🖋 Adapt your 3-Step Start to their Tribal Type.

🖋 Address the prospect by name, and then ask a question.

- Confirm the time and agenda. Be ready and able to reschedule if necessary.

- Research better connection questions for each prospect.

- Ask open-ended questions to connect and get them talking early.

- Remember to use proper Pause Time.

- Use active listening. Don't just plan what you're going to say next. Pause to respond once you've heard Them.

- Paraphrase what they said.

- Earn the right to move to the *Investigate* step.

- Remember to ask for permission to move from personal to business.

Success!

I met with one of the few female Field Consultants in the greater geographic area. We built rapport over time given our shared Arizona hometown connection. She is more of an Expresser and Achiever Tribal Type, in my opinion.

I reached out and scheduled lunch to continue to build rapport. At our lunch, I used the 3-Step Start:

Greet = Connect by discussing what's new with her and us.

Explain = Share the goal to see what's working for her and how we can help.

Ask = Questions to build off her thoughts on our solutions, find out if she is just looking for more success with SCHW internal solutions lately, and determine if she will consider us for the event.

Outcome? She extended a referral.

–GEORGE HAAS, CAPITAL ADVISORS

CHAPTER 24

Investigate: Investigation or Interrogation?

"Talk to people about themselves
and they will listen for hours."

—Benjamin Disraeli

After *Initiating* the two-way information exchange, you've earned the right to transition to the part of the conversation everyone talks about: discovery! Or, in the WIIFT® System, the *Investigate* step.

The *Investigate* step makes space within the conversation to discover and gather information. But not just any information—we need the prospect's "story." Knowing their story allows us to discover not only relevant data and details but also their POWNs.

To get into this collaborative discovery, you can easily segue from listening to their responses to your connection questions and then starting the *Investigation*. Use comments such as, "It is good to hear that you enjoy your job. Are you ready to move to the specific questions I have for you today?" or "I understand you are pressed for time, let's get to the reason we're talking."

This subtle approach to the conversation differentiates you from the competition and sets you up to collaboratively and productively *Investigate* the prospect's POWNs. When they have let you in and engaged in the conversation with you, it's a good start to collaboration.

I've heard advisors say, "All I need to do is get them talking." But don't be fooled into thinking that's all you need to do. That's not enough; the prospect needs to share relevant information and you need to actively listen, clarify with follow-up questions, add context to your questions, and adapt the questions as needed to keep the conversation collaborative. These are the nuances that will be covered in Chapter 27.

Filling out the *Investigate* section in the QPT guides you to identify the information that you and they need to uncover and to write the anchor questions that will uncover that information. So, make sure to prepare. Then following the guidelines laid out in the following chapters increases your ability to *Investigate* effectively, efficiently, and collaboratively, making you more valuable to your prospect as they make a decision.

A productive *Investigation* also qualifies the prospect and clarifies their motivations, gives a sense of urgency in addressing their POWNs, and earns us the right to then connect our service to their POWNs and the value of working together.

This is what we want. To get that productive *Investigation*, it needs to be collaborative, creating an experience of being "in it" together, not an interrogation with direct, pointed questions focused on a specific topic or course of action, creating an "us versus them" experience. While I haven't seen any advisor literally shine a bright light on unsuspecting people to pressure them into answering questions, sometimes the advisors ask questions that create that kind of experience.

The prospect experience matters, as we discussed in the *Initiate* chapters. And people who may already not feel great about their circumstances value an open, nonjudgmental exchange of information.

The Investigate Step Overview

A successful *Investigation* is assured when you meet the Objectives (the whys) for this discovery by effectively completing the 5 Actions (how-tos) listed below.

 Objectives

- ✓ Qualify the person and the company
- ✓ Broaden the conversation beyond the product/service
- ✓ Learn about the Problems, Opportunities, Wants, and Needs (POWNs) to determine if there is a gap
- ✓ Determine the level of urgency for POWNs
- ✓ Demonstrate interest and expertise

 Actions/How-tos

1. Ask relevant open-ended questions to discover POWNs guided by the 4-Point Investigation®
2. Listen actively
3. Ask follow-up questions
4. Paraphrase what They have stated
5. Qualify and confirm that They want to discuss a solution before moving on

Uncover Problems, Opportunities, Wants, and Needs

Now, before I introduce the Anchor framework of the *Investigate* step, let's explore what we are looking to uncover: POWNs.

Unlike sales advice you may have heard, digging for "pain" is not the only point of *Investigating*. Instead, expand your (and their) focus by helping the prospect *discover* and us to *uncover* their POWNs. This broader approach allows you to uncover potential opportunities to add value.

As we listen to the prospect's story, we need to uncover, and even help them discover, their POWNs.

- *Uncover the Problems* that are hurting or hindering the prospect in some way. This is the "pain" or problem that is making them uncomfortable enough to seek a solution to alleviate it. But some-times they have a hard time discussing their problems because they feel embarrassed or ashamed about it. They may also worry that discussing their problems makes them vulnerable to being "sold to." If selling is your main focus, you risk alienating them. In other cases, the prospect may not even recognize a problem or isn't open to addressing existing ones—for example, the prospect with 95% of their investments in Amazon stock who won't diversify.

- *Uncover the Opportunities* your prospects are dreaming of, don't know about, or have no idea how to capitalize on. Get them talking about what they wish for, how they would like things to be, and what ideas they have. Use your expertise, demonstrated through questions, to discuss opportunities they may not be aware of.

- *Uncover your prospects' Wants.* What your prospects want may be more powerful than what they need. Since wants are tied to emotions, they often feel a sense of urgency to fulfill their want. This emotional want is often the deciding factor, which they then justify with needs and facts.

✪ *Uncover your prospects' Needs.* What do they need to do, have, stop, or start? What must happen or be acquired? They may need a virtual relationship with email and texting communication only, advice on a specific financial situation, or a certain type of action or transaction completed. Not everybody has a specific need—or thinks they have one—which may mean that they would waste their time reviewing your service.

I'm often asked, "What's the difference between a want and a need?" An advisor I know explained it this way: "I may need a vehicle, but I want a Ferrari." A need is a necessity. A want is most often a desire or emotionally driven need.

When you discuss more than problems or needs with your prospects, you uncover more areas to add and attach value. For instance, a firm shared information with me about their current sales training program. They mentioned how comfortable they were facilitating the sessions, how the developer had customized the course for them 5 years earlier, and how satisfied they were with their current process. All their responses suggested they had no problem or need for my solution—a training course on collaborative selling.

Then I asked how they leveraged the time and money of their current program to sharpen the skills gained during the original seminar. They explained they spent considerable personal time creating reinforcing activities, messages, and support materials. That was my opportunity opener!

I focused on their unacknowledged needs—an opportunity to reduce their personal efforts—as we explored the value they would find in having such items developed for them. We were able to collaborate on the possibilities and potential implementation and timing of my training. The buy decision was made within a week.

The way you phrase your questions and explore problems or opportunities affects the responses you receive. I'll share more on the how-tos of asking questions in the next chapter.

Potential POWNS for Financial Services

The POWNs acronym ensures that you know *what* you need to know and what they may need to discover in the *Investigate* step.

Here are some POWNs thought-starters to get you thinking.

Problems to solve

🖎 Dealing with past poor financial decisions due to lack of knowledge

🖎 Trying to navigate equity comp decisions, including tax strategies for exercising and selling, alone

🖎 Reducing high tax rates

🖎 Making retirement planning decisions, such as withdrawals and insurance

🖎 Creating transparency on current investments

🖎 Needing a new advisor due to relationship breakdown with previous advisor

🖎 Seeking accountability for taking personal action on personal matters

🖎 Delaying in making important financial decisions

🖎 Dealing with an inheritance tax burden

Opportunities to capture

🖎 Becoming more organized

🖎 Improving transparency on where "all the money is"

🖎 Finding a thought partner to bounce financial ideas off of

🖎 Leaning on expertise in a finance niche

🖎 Coordinating and monitoring estate planning, accessing, and updating estate planning

- Identifying specific investing opportunities
- Understanding their financial situation
- Taking full advantage of income and assets
- Protecting assets from unnecessary taxes—inheritance, equity comp, gains, business, etc.
- Answering questions based on life stage: when, how much, what to do
- Mitigating business sales taxes

Wants prospects may have for financial services

- Feeling valued as a human
- Converting all documents into a specific format (print, digital, in the cloud)
- Accessing accounts easily
- Finding more time to focus on life pursuits—family, hobbies, philanthropy
- Becoming less overwhelmed
- Finding a holistic or comprehensive financial approach
- Creating a consistent income
- Ending worry or stress about money
- Gaining confidence in their financial decisions
- Living within their means now and during retirement years
- Finding a one-stop place for all finance matters
- Finding a preferred service model

Needs prospects may have

- Creating a plan that gets them to their goals
- Finding an advisor that serves their geographic location or matches their communication preferences
- Affording financial services
- Fixing tax problems
- Seeking specific expertise in a topic or situation
- Creating a specific growth strategy for their portfolio
- Establishing legacy goals
- Stabilizing cash flow
- Finding confidence to take the next step: retirement, moving on, etc.

Look at the list of possibilities for adding value! It's why I am so committed to helping you be more effective in your sales conversations. People need you!

POWNs are important, and they will make more sense to you and them when viewed from a framework of discovering their "story," as explained in the next chapter.

CHAPTER 25

The Investigate Step Anchor

Focus on surfacing key information that helps the
prospect move forward in the sales process and
make their first important decision: to work with you!

—A Nancy Timely Tip

Imagine you have finished your *Investigation* with a potential prospect and it's time to provide your recommendation or proposal. As you work on the recommendation and plan your next conversation, you realize you don't have all the information you really need. Sound familiar? This happens too often!

Or maybe, as you describe your services, you can't connect the service value to the client's POWNs specifically enough for the prospective client to see their relevance. And they lose interest.

It's easy to get caught thinking "I have enough information, and now it's time to tell them what I have or how I can help them." Premature recommendations, though, lead to extra follow-up activities, stalled opportunities, and possible frustration for you and the prospect.

It's also easy to collect too much information! Yes, it is possible to collect unnecessary information, which can obscure the information needed to make a confident, value-filled recommendation. This is why the anchor, a 4-Point Investigation™, is so helpful. It ensures you collect the right information.

Action 1: Ask Relevant, Open-Ended Questions Using the 4-Point Investigation

Graphic 25-1

Graphic 25-1 shows the framework of the 4-Point Investigation. The 4-Points will guide you to ask questions that will prompt the prospect to fully illuminate their situation, their story. The framework also allows you to identify whether you can provide what they need.

Before explaining the 4-Points, let's look at the first part of this Action: Ask relevant, open-ended questions.

Open-ended questions will solicit more information than closed questions. Open-ended questions draw out facts, emotions, motivations, and the degree of urgency. The right questions also solicit great information, get the person talking and clarifying their situation, show your expertise and professionalism, and allow you both to identify potential opportunities.

Closed questions ask the prospect for one piece of information or data. They narrow the focus of the conversation. "Do you have a problem with your _____?" is a direct closed question that may lead to qualifying the prospect, but it doesn't lead to an open collaborative conversation.

But what are the *relevant* questions that give you only the needed information and nothing more? To identify relevant questions, first determine what you need to learn and what your prospect needs to discover.

For example, you need to determine if they are a qualified prospect, and they may need to discover or clarify that they have POWNs and define their impact. When you clearly understand the information that needs to be discovered and uncovered, you can more easily develop effective potential questions to ask.

Open-ended questions begin with words like "who," "what," "how," and "why":

- What would happen if _____?
- What approach would you use to _____?
- How would you _____?
- What is the relationship between _____?
- What evidence have you found that _____?
- What could be changed or improved in _____?
- Where do you see _____?
- How do you select (or decide) _____?
- How do you prioritize _____?
- What information would be helpful when _____?

You can also request information with these starter statements:

- Please tell me about _____.
- Help me understand _____.
- Please share with me _____.

These *Investigation* thought-starters help prospects discover and discuss important information you will need to connect your solution to their POWNs.

TIMELY TIP

CAUTION! Although starting questions with "why" can help you uncover reasons and get explanations, it can also seem interrogative, aggressive, and manipulative in a sales conversation.

Use "why" only after trust is established and if your conversation is collaborative.

The 4-Point Framework

Now let's look closer at the framework to collect the most relevant information: their story.

The 4-Point Investigation framework (Graphic 25-1) helps you and your prospects cohesively explore the *facts* of Today and Tomorrow and the *emotional* and *logical* aspects of Risks and Rewards, positioning you as a collaborator who "gets it." Its structure allows you to collect the right information.

The revolving center in the graphic shows that an Investigation can go in many directions. The Point where you begin your investigation doesn't matter. What matters is that you connect and cover all four points.

Where do you start? Often the prospect's first comments direct your conversation to begin at one point or another. They might start by discussing what they want or need. Or they may start talking about their frustrations Today or the vision they have for Tomorrow. They also might openly discuss the fears or Risks they are concerned about or the benefits or Rewards they seek from you, your product, or your service.

Track what they share, using the 4-Points as your guide, then ask questions that fill in the gaps of their story!

The following is a description of each of the 4-Points, along with thought-starter questions for you to build from. Tweak these questions to work in your situation. They have been curated through workshops with thousands of financial advisors and have been left intentionally vague or incomplete to allow you to personalize them. These are meant to start discussions. Follow-up questions will allow you to uncover more.

There is no set order to these questions. Rather, use them according to the context of each situation. This will demonstrate your expertise and relevancy. (See information on Intention in Chapter 26.)

Now let's look closer at the 4-Points!

4-Point Investigation™

Today questions

Today questions ask for the backstory of the prospect's current state. For the following Today thought-starters, I'll use Advisory Services and Wealth Management as the overall topic of the questions.

🖋 Please tell me what led you to seek a financial advisor. What brought you here today? What prompted you to schedule a meeting?

🖋 What's your process when deciding on _____?

🖋 Please help me understand some of the challenges you are facing with _____.

🖇 What are your expectations from a _____?

🖇 What do you most value in working with your advisor? What's missing that led you to look elsewhere?

🖇 Please tell me about the relationship you have with your current advisor.

🖇 When you have financial decisions to make, who do you include/ rely on in your thought process?

🖇 What firms or advisors have you considered in your search?

🖇 What is causing the biggest problem and why?

🖇 What are some of the best financial decisions you've made so far?

🖇 How have you typically made big financial decisions in the past?

🖇 What influences your financial decision-making?

🖇 How are you compensating your current financial professional?

🖇 Thinking about your current advisor relationships, how happy are you with the value for the fee?

4-Point Investigation™

Tomorrow questions

The gap between Today and Tomorrow is important because that is where your initial opportunity lies. If your solution can reduce or remove the gap between what is happening Today and where the prospect wants or needs to be Tomorrow, you have a viable prospect and a potential sale. To that end, Tomorrow questions, like the thought-starters below, ask the prospect to discuss and clarify what they want or need for the future:

- What are your future plans for _____?
- What are your priorities for _____? (fill in time frame)
- What capabilities do you wish _____ had?
- From what you've already told me, how do you envision _____?
- What kind of help do you need?
- What are you trying to achieve?
- How would you like _____ to happen going forward?
- What do you think will be the one-year impact of successfully working together?
- What will make you feel like/think that working together is beneficial?
- How can we remove some of your financial stress?
- What are 3 financial milestones you are looking to achieve?
- What are your key financial goals?

4-Point Investigation™

Risk questions

These explore the potential downsides to moving to Tomorrow or staying in Today. Exploring the Risk of doing nothing is an effective way to identify the sense of urgency around the situation. Risk questions, such as the thought-starters below, provide the prospect with powerful motivation to do something:

- What are you concerned might happen in _____?
- What might be the consequences if we take no action?
- What does that mean to your family?
- What will happen if you don't address _____?
- What are your concerns?
- What might be the risks of making a change now?
- What are the roadblocks you see in working toward your goals?
- What are your concerns about continuing to handle your own finances?
- When you think about working with a financial advisor, what concerns you?
- How will your life be affected if you don't get this taken care of?
- How will _____ affect how you think about _____?

4-Point Investigation™

Reward

Today • .

• Tomorrow

Risk

Reward questions

Reward questions explore the benefits prospects are looking for when Tomorrow is reached and the potential benefits of them staying in

Today. These questions, like the thought-starters below, help you understand the motivations that may drive the person to action and decision:

- How would using a financial plan to guide financial decisions provide clarity in your life?

- What benefits are you looking for by working with a financial advisor?

- Where would you spend more of your time, knowing you have a plan and support in place?

- What could you do with the time this will save you?

- What might you gain from having _____?

- How will your schedule improve if we make this change?

- How would having a detailed plan in place allow you to more fully enjoy your life?

- If we could look ahead 2 to 3 years, what would need to have changed to make working together considered a success?

- When you think about the future, what are some of the experiences, activities, and "things" you look forward to?

- How would this change help you reduce risk for _____?

You can also form Risk and Reward questions from the follow-up questions described in Chapter 27, Action 3 of the *Investigate* step.

Covering all points in a 4-Point Investigation keeps you from moving the conversation forward too soon and missing opportunities—for you and your prospect.

Your prospects might not expect you to gather their full story. Expanding the conversation starts with the expectations you set in the *Initiate* step and continues with the questions you ask during *Investigation* that just might open up opportunities to add massive value, as Brant Cavagnaro of Wealthstream Advisors did:

A sophisticated prospect with a background in financial services came into a large lump sum of cash and reached out to us in order to manage his assets. His initial goal was to have us simply invest his money. After asking more 4-Point questions during the initial call, it was uncovered that his estate documents were out of date, he didn't know his expenses, nor did he understand when he could exactly retire.

Discovering this information allowed us to explain how we could tackle these gaps in his financial plan and why a cash flow projection could provide clarity to several of his questions (how much to save, what is the appropriate amount of stocks vs. bonds, when could he retire, etc.). I believe he went into that initial call expecting us to wow him with investment jargon instead of trying to put the pieces of his financial puzzle together.

He ended up moving forward, initially investing $1.5 million, and has repeatedly said to us over the years that our financial planning pays for the fees itself and that he doesn't even care to look at his investments anymore.

Although the 4-Point Investigation framework is extremely helpful, it does not guarantee an easy *Investigation* with every prospect. Prospects generally have a comfort zone about what they are willing and ready to discuss. For this reason, knowing *what* to ask needs to be matched with *how* to ask questions they are willing and able to answer. That's why the next chapter will feature the "how-tos" of asking questions that *Investigate*, not interrogate.

CHAPTER 26

Investigate How-tos: Ask Questions Prospects Want to Answer

You may demonstrate your brilliance—or lack thereof—during the Investigation more than during the presentation of your solution!

—A Nancy Timely Tip

While the questions you ask using the 4-Point Investigation are important, *how* you ask the questions is equally so. Even open-ended questions, if used incorrectly, can make an *Investigation* seem like an interrogation. They can be leading, forced, narrow, you-focused, or irrelevant.

Advisors can come off as uncaring or only "focused on the money" when they drill a prospect. This has contributed to the negative connotation around financial selling, making your questions seem self-serving and uncollaborative. How do you instead appear curious and helpful as you ask questions? By being Intentional, Intelligent,

Interesting, and Indirect—what I like to call the four I's. Let's look at each of these in more detail.

Intentional Questions

Being Intentional in your *Investigation* means asking context questions. I've seen well-meaning advisors launch right into their list of prepared questions, and I've watched their prospects give them a look that says, "What's this have to do with anything?" or "Whoa, those are a little personal. What do they have to do with what I wanted to talk about?"

That's what happens when the prospect has no idea why these questions are being asked, what the advisor's intent is, or if they should really answer the questions.

On the other hand, when you "set up" and explain the purpose of your questions, the prospect has perspective, which means they can feel safe and answer more thoughtfully, allowing you to continue a collaborative conversation.

I received a sales call some time ago in which the caller immediately asked, "So, what are you working on?" My reply? "Wow, that's broad. In what context?" He responded, "Whatever context you choose." Well, I was confused. I knew this person was selling lead generation services, and I wondered whether he wanted me to answer based on that narrow interest or if he was really trying to find out more.

So, I turned it back to him and said, "What are *you* working on?" He responded in great detail about what he was doing and about his services. After 5 minutes I knew where he really wanted the conversation to go—to his solution—and I wasn't interested.

He asked questions without sharing his intent, which immediately put me on guard. So first, set up your intent, which may sound like this, especially when you personalize it:

"Now we'll look more specifically at your situation. We've noticed that when discussing experiences, goals, thoughts, and feelings around finances, it's important for us to hear from each of you so we can best support both of you. These first questions are focused on the broader picture. Then we'll get more specific."

Now the conversation moves into your list of open-ended, relevant questions.

It is also helpful to share the intent and context before each new topic. Here are a couple of examples:

"In working with couples nearing retirement, we've found it helpful to talk more about retirement goals and concerns."

"With our work with high-level professionals such as yourself, it's helpful to discuss your career and work goals."

Intelligent Questions

Intelligent questions draw from your experience and research. They differentiate you from the competition to show your expertise in a more subtle way and help you discover or clarify relevant information or situations in a timely way.

Prospects do not want their time wasted, and asking them irrelevant and common questions can make you sound like everyone else. So, you want to complete your research, think of the value your solutions bring to their situation, and know this prospect to help you find Intelligent questions.

Tips for asking Intelligent questions:

🖎 Research your prospects as discussed in Chapter 15.

🖎 Prepare a list of questions that will broaden the conversation beyond your product or service. For example, instead of asking "What kind of an issue do you have with _____?" ask, "In preparing for today and reading your responses to the scheduling questions, I've noticed that your _____ is a focus for you in the next several years. How does your _____ contribute to that focus?"

🐟 Know the value your solution provides versus just the features. For example, if you are a comprehensive financial planner, ask if they have an advisor already and what their impact has been: "Please share with me how working with your advisor has impacted this current situation."

🐟 Know your industry and competitors. This allows you to ask questions such as "How is the trend of _____ impacting your thoughts about your financial future?"

The questions asked during the *Investigate* step directly reflect your expertise on the topic of discussion. You may demonstrate your brilliance—or lack thereof—during the *Investigation* more than during the presentation of your solution!

 TIMELY TIP

A caution about Intelligent questions: Be careful that you do not use industry jargon—acronyms and terms—that the prospect may not be familiar with, like the famous "F" word: fiduciary.

If they feel "dumb" or uninformed, they may shut down the conversation. No one likes a show-off. Gauge the prospect's expertise and knowledge, and adjust your questions accordingly.

Indirect Questions

Indirect questions draw out the intent, emotions, and preferences of the prospect. They introduce deeper, more pointed questions in a softer way.

Say your prospect is planning a vacation. A vacation planner could ask questions like:

- "How many people are in your family?"
- "What's your budget?"
- "Where do you want to go?"
- "Who will be traveling?"
- "What are your dates of travel?"
- "What airline do you prefer?"
- "Why do you want to stay in this location?"

Notice the tone of this series of questions. They begin with how, what, where, who. And at first, they appear to be open-ended, yet they are really closed and direct. They lead directly to narrow specific information responses.

A vacation planner would likely find more success by asking questions like:

- "Tell me about the type of vacation you want to take."
- "What is your travel experience?"
- "What type of activities do you want to include in your trip?"
- "What is your budget?"
- "Who will be traveling with you?"
- "What places do you want to explore as options? Which do you want to stay away from?"
- "How many days do you have available for travel?"
- "What concerns do you have about traveling outside the country?"
- "What is one thing you want to experience?"

Notice how these questions ask for information, not just data. The responses to the second series of questions would allow the vacation planner to collaboratively discuss options with the traveler.

Interesting Questions

Every aspect of the sales process should be WiifT focused, including your questions!

Make your questions Interesting by asking relevant questions about the situation and people involved. When it's about them, they'll be interested and more willing to share information and discuss how you can help them.

The information you gather during the *Wait* step's research about the prospect's family, career, and situation can be used to ask questions that interest them. You wouldn't ask an unmarried, successful 35-year-old the same questions in the same way as you would ask a married 63-year-old with a union pension. Their demographics, experiences, and POWNs are different—and the questions should reflect this.

Adjust Your Questions to the Tribal Types

To make the questions more Interesting, adjust your word choice and phrasing for the customs of each Tribal Type.

Commanders and Achievers often prefer "thinking" words in their questions:

- "Please share with me your thoughts about _____."
- "What do you think is creating _____?"

Reflectors and Expressers respond to "feeling" words in their questions:

- "How do you feel this will _____?"
- "How does your family prioritize _____?"

Here's an example from my own experience: I was working with a group of high-level financial professionals. At the end of an activity, I asked a woman, "How do you feel that activity worked for you?"

She stared blankly back at me. I waited for her response—5 seconds, 10 seconds—and then another participant said, "You asked a Commander a feeling question!"

I smiled and immediately restated the question: "Lisa, how do you *think* that activity worked for you?" She answered within moments.

Adjusting the questions to fit different Tribes isn't that difficult. Here's how to easily adjust a question about a prospect's priorities for each Tribal Type:

Commander: *What have you found are the top 3 financial areas that need review?*

Reflector: *Please explain the 3 areas of your financial situation that are most concerning.*

Expresser: *Help me understand the 3 areas that have the most potential for improvement.*

Achiever: *What are the top 3 financial areas you want to address?*

Notice how the questions seek the same information yet are phrased differently. Making your questions Interesting means they are relevant and adjusted for their Tribal Type's customs.

In addition to word choice, the prospect's Tribal Type factors into what information they want to focus on. The Commander and Achiever Tribes may be comfortable discussing problems and reviewing risks because they want to "fix" things. They want to address problems by tackling them head-on, so they don't get in the way of success.

This isn't always true for Expressers and Reflectors, who may want to explain things in a broader and softer way. Achievers and Expressers like to "dream" and are comfortable talking about opportunities. They are generally more open to risk and being early adopters of ideas and solutions. Discussing hopes, dreams, and possibilities energizes them.

Different phrasing and focus profoundly impact how easy your questions are to answer and how the experience plays out for the prospects, even if you are collaborating with multiple decision-makers. A personal example may shed light on this.

I supported my adult daughter, Jenna, in selecting and purchasing her home in 2021. She had a wonderful realtor named Abby. Abby asked Jenna, an inexperienced buyer who exhibits Reflector customs when making purchase decisions, wonderful questions to learn her story.

Early on in the buying process, Jenna and Abby easily began casually chitchatting about all kinds of topics: where Jenna hung out, what brought her to the area, and Abby also shared stories about her daughter, who is near Jenna's age. When they first met, they didn't seem to have a care in the world.

I, a time-strapped Achiever and experienced real estate buyer, wanted to get to the "real" questions on location, budget, safety needs, the market, availability, and the likelihood she could afford or even find a property in the currently crazy, competitive market. I knew Abby was trying to build rapport and "connect" with Jenna, but I had a schedule to keep and wanted us to look at properties quickly; new listings often went under contract within hours during the hot real estate market early in 2021!

Abby realized that I was an influencer and contributor in this decision—both emotionally and financially. She promptly moved the property search forward while continuing to bond with Jenna. Abby skillfully navigated the rest of the transaction with our two sets of buying needs by talking directly with Jenna and keeping me updated through texts and emails after she and Jenna had follow-up conversations. When she needed quick answers, she reached out to me first to get it done.

Her approach worked, and we were pleasantly surprised when Jenna "won" the first desirable property we looked at. The whole experience left both Jenna and me extremely satisfied with Abby, who knew how to work with two very different sets of buying customs!

There you have it: a lot of information about the first Action of Investigate: *Ask relevant, open-ended questions.* We've just covered the whats and how-tos of asking these questions, and yet that is just *one* skill to use in this part of the conversation. Great questions need a partner: great listening!

CHAPTER 27

Investigate: The Nuances That Make a Conversation Collaborative

Your follow-up questions indicate your level of interest and curiosity to understand the prospect's story.

—A Nancy Timely Tip

Asking good questions in a 4-Point Investigation is just one part of Investigating well. We also need the next Actions—the nuances for effective *Investigating*.

Action 2: Listen Actively

Active listening is something you do; it is not a passive endeavor. Active listening means you are involved, engaged, and present during the conversation. When you listen actively, you place your client at the center of the conversation, enabling the conversation to flow smoothly, with a continuous two-way exchange of information. Your ability and willingness to listen demonstrate that you are engaged with them and care about the information the prospect is sharing. To listen actively, use these tips:

- *Pay attention.* Use eye contact, eliminate distractions, and avoid multitasking.

- *Respond to what they say with sounds and movement.* Use "audibles" such as "okay," "interesting," and "hmmm" to show you are listening. Verbal responses are especially necessary in telephone conversations.

- *Watch for signals that show their intent and emotion.* These signals may include body language, tone, and pace.

- *Remain open to their responses* and hear their full answer before judging or responding.

- *Take notes.* Taking notes not only creates a reference for later but also slows your mind down in the moment so you listen better. Many advisors have quickly adopted AI to help with this, as it makes note-taking and writing follow-up emails easier.

The actual skill of listening isn't usually the problem, though. What's usually more challenging is the discipline to talk less so that we can listen better. Often a "talking trigger," something that makes you talk more than you should or need to, takes over.

These triggers can be:

- Nervousness

- Lack of confidence

- The desire or need to prove ourselves

- Uncertainty as to where to go next in the conversation

- The desire to convince or talk someone into something

- Not having been trained to listen!

To listen better, prepare for your conversations. (Yes, preparation is so critical in effective collaboration that I'm going to reinforce it over and over again.) Identify your personal talking trigger and eliminate it with proper preparation. And use the Pause Time strategies introduced in Chapter 21 after asking each question. Sometimes, just forcing yourself to listen rather than talk—even if it's to ask great questions—works well.

Years ago, a client, Rick, referred me to a prospect. During the one-hour telephone sales call, I kept my focus on the prospect. I asked questions that I had prepared and forced myself to listen as I took notes and made verbal sounds of paying attention—*uh huh, oh,* and *hmmm.* I also paraphrased his responses.

When he had an interruption and needed to end the call early, I asked to speak with him again, and he agreed. I hung up and then thought, "Oh, that was a waste of time. I never got a chance to explain anything to him, and he has no idea what I do or how I can help him." The following day, Rick asked about the call. As I was about to share my concerns about not getting a chance to really converse, he blurted, "Well, whatever you did, he thought you were brilliant!" I'll take that win!

When you actively listen and focus all your attention on the prospect—pausing and stopping your triggers from setting your mouth in motion—your prospect will think *you* are brilliant and want to continue the conversation.

Your ability, skill, and attitude toward listening are equally as important as asking the right questions. The combination of asking for the right information, hearing what they tell you, and then presenting a solution that addresses their POWNs wins sales.

Action 3: Ask Follow-Up Questions

To keep the responses yielding important and more specific information, add follow-up questions in your *Investigation.* After asking an anchored, open-ended question, seek information by asking 1 or 2 follow-up questions is extremely effective.

Ask follow-up questions to seek further context, clarity, and intent:

- ⌇ "That's interesting. Please tell me more about _____."
- ⌇ "I understand that _____ is your priority this year. How does that impact _____?"
- ⌇ "I've heard similar things from other prospects. How do you see _____?"
- ⌇ "It seems that _____. What would you add or clarify?"
- ⌇ "Let's look at that closer please."
- ⌇ "I'd like to hear more about this. Can you expand a bit further?"

Risk and Reward questions also make good follow-up questions:

- ⌇ "What do you think the impact of that will be?"
- ⌇ "Who else will be affected by this _____ (situation, problem, information)?"
- ⌇ "What happens because _____?"
- ⌇ "How does _____ affect?"

Your follow-up questions indicate your level of interest and curiosity to understand the prospect's story.

Action 4: Paraphrase What the Prospect Has Stated

Paraphrasing is powerful. Paraphrasing is not word-for-word repeating what the prospect shared with you; that is parroting. Instead, paraphrasing means summarizing their intent and "story" in your own words.

Knowing that you will paraphrase—both words and intent—keeps you focused, shows prospects you have heard them, and allows them to hear a summary of their own messages. After they hear your paraphrase, it's not uncommon for the prospect to clarify or explain certain points, which helps both of you.

But at some point, the questioning needs to lead to discussing the solution and getting a decision from them. To determine if it's time to move to the next step of the WIIFT System, summarize the information you have compiled and then complete the last Action for *Investigate*: further qualifying your prospect.

Action 5: Qualify and Confirm Your Opportunity

Qualify that They want to discuss a solution before moving on. Confirm that the prospect is willing and able to make a decision at the right time, that they have the fee tolerance, and that they want to *do* something to address their POWNs. Additionally, qualify the prospect to ensure they are a fit for you, your services, and your service model.

🔊 To qualify and confirm, start with a statement or segue such as: "Now that we have a good understanding of your situation ..."

Then ask:

🔊 "Before we go on, who else should be included in our conversation?"

🔊 "What's your plan for selecting a firm?"

🔊 "What's your timing for looking at solutions?"

TIMELY TIP

It's easy to assume that someone who has shared information with you must want to act on that information. Not true! Before investing time and effort in collaborating about recommendations, confirm that they are open to a solution and ask about their timing. It will help you prioritize where to spend your time and energy.

Couple Investigations

Extracting information from a couple requires extra effort because of the additional variables involved. You've probably experienced many of them. Each partner may have a different Tribal Type as well as different priorities, sense of urgency, level of interest, level of knowledge, and level of commitment. To increase your probability of gathering good information with a couple or group, use these strategies:

- Provide questions for them to discuss in advance of your conversation.
- During the conversation, ask each person for a response to the most important questions.
- Pay attention to body language to spot who may have something to say but is not speaking up.
- Explain that if one person has more questions, you're happy to share additional information after the conversation if needed.
- Ask for information in different ways to resonate with the different Tribal Types.
- If one person is dominating the discussion, direct follow-up questions to the other using their name: "Thank you, Anne. That was very helpful. Steve, what can you add to the information Anne shared?"

* * * * *

A complete *Investigation* may seem cumbersome and lengthy. Yet it doesn't need to be. Depending on your sales process, 3 or 4 anchor questions, with added follow-up questions, may be all you need to initially discover a prospect's POWNs, qualify the prospect, and move to the next step. Other sales processes may include several conversations.

Each prospect's situation is unique. Your preparation and ability to *Investigate* POWNs with your prospect earns you the right to advance your sales conversation to the *Facilitate* step.

CHAPTER 28

Investigate Quick Tips and Best Practices

As you implement the *Investigate* step, use these quick tips and best practices, from advisors who have completed the Genuine Sales 12-week course. There's also a success story to show the concepts in action.

Quick Tips

🌀 Ask relevant, open-ended questions within the 4-Point Investigation to surface their story. Ask for information about Today and Tomorrow and about Risk and Reward (the impact).

🌀 Use the thought-starter questions provided to create a list of 8-10 anchor questions.

🌀 Adjust your questions to each Tribal Type. Use "thinking" words in the questions for Commanders and Achievers and "feeling" words for Expressers and Reflectors.

🌀 Listen actively. Nod your head, verbalize that you hear the prospect, and focus on their responses.

🅢 Pay attention to your listening habits. Determine if they are effective and, if not, set a goal to make incremental changes to listen more.

🅢 Ask follow-up questions. Clarify the prospect's responses and seek more information.

🅢 Make a list of "go to" follow-up questions to shortcut your prep and pull them out "in the moment."

🅢 Paraphrase their story. Summarize—don't parrot back. Capture the emotions and context as well as the key facts.

🅢 Qualify the prospect before moving to the *Facilitate* step or recommending a solution. Ask about their decision-making process, where they are in the process, their timing, and who else will be involved in making the decision.

Advisor's Best Practices and Tips for Investigating

🅢 Create a 4-Point question chart based on each Tribal Type.

🅢 Ask 2 or 3 follow-up questions for clarification.

🅢 Paraphrase and repeat anything you didn't understand.

🅢 Understand the journey that brought them to the conversation.

🅢 Pause to give them time to respond to questions or to take notes.

🅢 Prep questions ahead of time.

🅢 Ask questions from the Today, Tomorrow, Risk, and Reward categories.

🅢 Make sure your questions are open-ended and you ask different types of questions.

🅢 Pay attention to your listening habits.

🅢 Ask intelligent questions that are relevant to your prospect's needs.

🡆 Actively work to include a qualify-and-confirm question.

🡆 When working with a couple, purposefully involve both people.

Success!

I signed on a new client that will generate $6K in annual fees because I focused on uncovering their POWNs and then customizing my offering to their POWNs. I also gained four ongoing clients by using the Investigate step and Whats to WiifTs.

–ZHI LI, TWELVE TWO CAPITAL LLC

CHAPTER 29

Facilitate and Make it Easy for Them to "Get It": An Overview

> "Everything should be made as simple as possible, but not simpler."
>
> —Albert Einstein

Facilitate means to make it easier, or less difficult, for something to be accomplished.

What a plan! Instead of pitching or presenting, you can *Facilitate* the ongoing information exchange and make it easy for them to see how your solution matters to them.

It's tough to hire a financial advisor. There's nothing tangible to hold, it's hard to compare outcomes from other advisors, there is no "money back guarantee," and most people don't have a lot of experience in hiring finance professionals.

That's why the easier we make the prospect's decision process, the more efficiently and confidently they can make that decision. One of our goals in "selling" should be to make everything as easy as possible for them! And that's why we use the word *Facilitate* in the WIIFT® Sales System.

After learning their story in the *Investigate* step, the *Facilitate* step is where you help Them easily connect how your solution specifically addresses their POWNs. It's not as much show and tell as it is collaborate and sell, as you fully demonstrate your solution and expertise.

Watch out for potential traps at this point of the conversation. Too little information shared or too much information not directly connected to their POWNs quickly kills your sales opportunity. Applying the how-tos for *Facilitate* allows you to "right size" and avoid overtelling or underselling.

While the *Facilitate* step will be explained as a standalone step, in the real world, *Investigate* and *Facilitate* are blended. Often you *Facilitate* some information in the setup to your questions. Or following a prospect's discussion of a specific POWN to be addressed, a short affirmative comment or example that allows the prospect to know they are talking to the right person.

What's important as you *Facilitate* the information sharing of your solution is that you demonstrate value and include Them to continue to collaborate.

This focus on Them carries all the way through solutioning, including working through any concerns, objections, potential barriers, or next steps, together.

There are different formats to *Facilitate* this value connection:

🖎 Formal presentation to a person or group

🖎 Conversations on video, in-person, or through email

🖎 Written proposal or recommendation

The Facilitate Step Overview

 ### Objectives

✓ Identify the value they will receive.
✓ Help someone else get on board—their spouse, partner, or anyone "on" their team.
✓ Provide the right information to quickly receive or implement the solution.
✓ Aid the prospect in making a decision.
✓ Collaborate through concerns or questions.

After the hard work of discovering the POWNs, it's time to make it easy to connect what you have with what they need!

 ### Actions/How-tos

1. Explain your solution with Whats to WiifTs.
2. Include others in the information delivery and ask for feedback.
3. Provide proof to support you and your solution.
4. Present costs followed by value.
5. Ask for and work through concerns with Stop, Drop, and Roll.

The Actions of this step work in all modes of conversations: : one-on-one, couples, face-to-face, virtual, telephone, webinars, seminars, and even in official presentations. They are divided into 2 parts. The first 4 *Facilitate* Actions are discussed collectively in the next chapters.

The second part starts in Chapter 34 to detail the last Action of *Facilitate*, working through concerns as a problem solver.

CHAPTER 30

Facilitate, Part I: Create Collaborative Solution Presentations Focused on the Prospect

Don't assume your prospects will "get" the value for them. It takes energy, effort, and knowledge to make these connections. It's your responsibility to make value obvious.

—A Nancy Timely Tip

Action 1: Explain Your Solution with Whats to WiifTs

The first Action is also the anchor, which can be used any time you share or explain information. When you find yourself explaining or sharing any information you can't connect to one of their POWNs, stop talking! If it's not relevant to them, you may inadvertently lose their attention.

Any information you share becomes more powerful when you connect the information to Them. They'll listen, care, and "get" the value to them.

It's a simple premise: explain *what* your solution has or what it does and connect it to the benefits or *What's in it for Them*. I call these "Whats to WiifTs."

The how-to is seemingly easy: connect *anything* you share to their POWNs and relate it to their story, the 4-Points. Show them how your solution moves them from Today to Tomorrow while minimizing Risks and maximizing their Rewards.

Whats to WiifTs makes it easy for your prospects to make the feature-to-benefit connection and ensures that they understand the value of your solution. This is where your knowledge and experience come into play.

If you leave it to them to make the value connection, they likely will not have the knowledge, experience, or context to do so. That's why when you only present the features or process of your solution, prospects can get distracted, become indifferent, start feeling that they are being sold to, and, worse, miss the value of your solution. Don't assume the value for them is obvious. It takes energy, effort, and knowledge to make these connections. By assuming this responsibility, we make it easy for them to make the connection.

What + WiifT = Value

"Whats to WiifTs" sounds like this:

⚑ "Working together, we'll look at all aspects of your financial picture so you can confidently select your retirement date."

⚑ "We'll apply our expertise in taxes to ensure that your tax liabilities are as low as possible each year."

How to Make the What to WiifT Connection

To make the What to WiifT connection, state the What (feature or detail of your service, process, firm, credentials, etc.) and connect it to the WiifT (benefit or outcome).

The challenge for most advisors typically isn't knowing enough information or Whats; the challenge is right-sizing what you know to sort through your brain's huge database and extract the most relevant Whats— those that directly address the prospect's POWNs.

For example, if your service is comprehensive financial planning and investment management and the prospect's POWNs are focused on retirement planning, details about your expertise in student loan planning or 529 plans aren't what's most important. Sharing those now can distract the prospect from seeing the value you can provide. And worse, it may lead them to think they should have discounted fees, as they won't access those areas of your service immediately.

Essentially, as you share each What, the prospect is thinking, "What does this have to do with me?" Imagine a "So What?" sign blinking on their forehead as they look at you. To make the sign disappear, connect a relevant WiifT to the What by including phrases with "you" and "your":

⚑ We'll assist you in getting all your estate planning finalized, which will make sure *you and your heirs avoid paying unnecessary taxes.*

⚑ We include comprehensive life planning in our work with you so that **you** have clarity on your family goals and priorities.

🖋 In working together, we will identify your risk tolerance, which allows **you** to build a portfolio that is invested in the right areas to support **you** achieving the desired returns.

🖋 The annual financial review includes a comprehensive report of your investment accounts which will *save you time during year-end tax preparation.*

🖋 As we manage your investments, we invest your extra cash with your business in mind, which allows **you** *to maximize your earnings from your profits!*

Doing this tells the prospect, "Hey, pay attention, this is about you!"

Below are some connecting phrase options that lead to the WiifT detail:

🖋 For **your** situation ...

🖋 What this means for **you** ...

🖋 So **you** will be able to ... or, So that you ...

🖋 This allows **you** to ...

🖋 In **your** situation, this means that ...

You will find the connection phrases that sound and feel right to you as you put this into play. Not only does personalizing your phrases keep you from sounding phony and rehearsed, it also allows you to vary the way you explain the information throughout your conversation.

This framework is flexible. Mix it up by also sharing WiifTs connected to Whats: "You mentioned that you have urgent needs when buying real estate, and you'll find that our availability will support those needs."

To prepare your most common Whats to WiifTs, you can duplicate this chart and fill in the topics/information you share. Strive to ask yourself "So What?" at least twice (ideally four times!).

What	So what?	WiifT	So what?	WiifT	So what?	WiifT

Your answers to the "So Whats?" will allow you to share powerful, relevant WiifT statements for different prospect situations. Remember, you identify the WiifT by stating how your solution solves the problem, captures opportunities for them, fills their wants and needs, and ties into their specific situation. The QPT prompts you to do just this. Make the time to prepare the information you most often share, then practice making the connection.

Here's an example of how that might look:

What	So what?	WiifT	So what?	WiifT	So what?	WiifT
Tax loss harvesting		Lowers your tax burden		Pay Uncle Sam less and keep more money in your pocket		Have that money for what matters most to you. For example, give more to kids, use for a vacation, or for college

What	So what?	WiifT	So what?	WiifT	So what?	WiifT
Risk tolerance assessment		Helps you understand your investment style		You'll be more comfortable with your level of risk tolerance and can better withstand market fluctuations		You avoid making rash decisions and improve your overall financial performance

CHAPTER 31

Facilitate: The Nuances of Making It Easy

Facilitating is not as much show
and tell as it is collaborate and sell.

—A Nancy Timely Tip

Making it easy is the focus of all collaborative selling efforts. And especially in the *Facilitate* step of WIIFT!

How much should you talk during this part of the conversation? While there is some research on this, I don't have exact percentages for you—there are too many variables in any sales situation to say that talking 67% of the time is the ideal. And which one of you wants to measure that for yourself? So just aim for a fifty-fifty talking to listening ratio. And that means the prospect must be involved and contributing!

Although the topic of discussion is now you and your service or solution, it's still not all about you; it's about you *and* Them. I can't stress this enough: in collaborative selling, it's a "we" dynamic from pre-start to post-finish.

You need to engage them collaboratively with healthy doses of inclusion. Research from the Sales Insights Lab found that top performers' conversations are much more engaging, dynamic, and back-and-forth with their prospects.[8]

Action 2: Include Others in the Information Delivery and Ask for Feedback

The style for sharing information about your solution using Whats to WiifTs can be a more formal or casual presentation. No matter which style fits the relevant information you're sharing, this part of the conversation should continue to be a time of two-way communication.

As you explain your process and service, apply Whats to WiifTs and keep it collaborative with conscious actions every 3–4 minutes, as outlined in the nuances of *Facilitate*.

Let me illustrate the importance of including your prospects in your delivery of information. For this example, please put yourself in the mode of a buying customer right now. Suppose you decide to purchase a new sofa. The furniture showroom advisor does a great job of *Investigating* your POWNs and points out your sofa options. They then lead you to the service counter and ask, "Which sofa do you think will best suit you?"

How would you feel? Would you be ready to select your sofa and make the purchase? Probably not.

You weren't involved in the review of your options or allowed to sit on the sofas to determine how they fit you or to compare different

---

[8]   Marc Wayshak, "23 Surprising New Sales Statistics for 2023 from Our Groundbreaking Studies!," Sales Insights Lab, January 3, 2022, https://salesinsightslab.com/sales-research/.

sofas. You were robbed of the opportunity to select the right one for you and to start mentally picturing one in your home.

What if, instead, the furniture expert follows their *Investigation* with an approach like this:

"From what you told me, comfort and color are the two most important considerations for you. What else is important to you? (Pause for response.) Let's look at your options and give you time to sit and recline on different sofas, and when you find the sofa that feels right, we'll look at color options. Most of our pieces can be custom ordered in dozens of fabrics. Let's start over here."

Then you spend time sitting on sofas, reviewing the different options, and selecting a fabric while continuing to talk with the advisor about what you like and don't like about the sofas you've been shown.

The furniture rep then says, "It looks like we have found the right fit for comfort and the color that is right for your room. What questions or concerns do you have about that sofa?"

How would you feel now? Would you be ready to continue the conversation and explore whether this is the right sofa for you?

The chances are much higher that you would continue, aren't they?

It's the same with your prospects. They don't want to be passive subjects when learning about and reviewing your solution and its fit to their POWNs—they want to get their hands (and all senses) on it!

Passive prospects "watching" your delivery can flip into the mode of discriminating prospects: "I tell you what I think I want, and then sit back and judge or dismiss your suggestions or solution." When they aren't a part of the solution, it is easier for them to be a detached judge and jury.

Collaboratively Involve Your Prospect

To include your prospects and continue to collaborate, first, invite Them to participate! A starter comment such as, "Let's explore how working together will address _____ (fill in the blank with

POWNs). Please ask any questions along the way." By setting this expectation, you continue the two-way information exchange.

Involve as many senses as possible, whether your conversation is face-to-face, virtual, on the telephone, or in a couple selling situation. What can you get their hands on? Eyes looking at? Head thinking about? Heart connecting to? And their mouth providing feedback and further information about?

Engage their *minds* with stories or examples. Explain how your solution addresses their POWNs or how it has solved POWNs for other people. If they are an Expresser or Reflector, share a short story that includes the background, action, and outcome. For Achievers and Commanders, share a more fact-based example without all the color, and be sure to nail the outcome or result!

You can also engage their minds with a discussion of best practices. Prospects want to know what others are doing that works well. Explain the best practices, how-tos, and specifics of not only your solution's results but also how other prospects have implemented the solution and other best practices around it.

Engage their *hands and eyes*:

🖘 *Provide hands-on items.* Put something in their hands—a paper, the mouse, or a pen—whenever possible. You can involve their hands by having them click on web pages or hold a document.

🖘 *Use overviews and samples.* I've seen everything from one-page plans to a large financial map used effectively in the delivery of information and demonstration of initial recommendations.

🖘 *Use of visual aids.* PowerPoint slides, written materials, screen sharing, and videos are all powerful tools to help the prospect learn about your solution and the WiifT. Use diagrams, analogies, and metaphoric imagery to make a point, draw a correlation, and show the potential benefits. The key is to turn these aids into tools that make it more about Them and less about you; use these tools to demonstrate what you do and what it can do for Them.

When preparing your QPT, don't bypass the opportunity to identify viable inclusion ideas in the section on *Facilitate* to get their hands, eyes, head, heart, and mouth involved.

One of the easiest ways to keep Them involved is to continue to provide openings for Them to talk and share their thoughts, opinions, and questions through what I call Feedback Questions.

Ask Feedback Questions

You can ask feedback questions effectively as you share Whats to WiifTs about your solution. Regularly pause and seek the prospect's viewpoint, opinions, and feelings about the fit of the solution to their POWNs and expectations.

Tap into their experiences and expertise to discover and discuss the benefits and challenges of your solution, explore their opinion, and collaborate on how to implement what you offer. Educated prospects will appreciate the chance to highlight their knowledge. Novice financial prospects may have many questions, and it's easier to address them along the way than wait until the end.

The prospects' responses to feedback questions often reward you with additional information about their intent, sense of urgency, and POWNs. It's a continuation of the *Investigation*—remember, I said that the steps blend.

Of course, it's possible that asking for feedback could produce negative information or unrealistic expectations. That's okay, though, because you can use this as an opportunity to circle back in WIIFT to further explore or clarify their POWNs.

Feedback questions keep Them engaged, save time, identify objections and concerns early, and redirect the conversation back to the *Investigate* step if the recommendation or solution is not a fit.

The following examples of feedback questions encourage your prospect to share useful information:

- "How does this match up with what you were considering?"
- "How do you see this moving you toward your goals?"
- "What is the best part of what we have discussed?"
- "Where do you see this fitting in with your priorities?"
- "How would this help alleviate the hurt feelings you're experiencing around money decisions?"
- "How do you see this helping you reach your _____ goal?"
- "Which part of these services do you find would be beneficial to help you?"

Listen to their initial feedback and then clarify, if necessary, with additional follow-up questions:

- "That's interesting. Tell me more."
- "You make a good point. How else can you see this working?"
- "What other ideas do you have?"
- "Tell me what you think about _____."
- "How do you feel about _____?"

Prospects begin to sell themselves as they collaboratively discuss possibilities and share their feedback. Your final service option, implementation, timeline, and terms are often better when discussed and developed collaboratively.

Tap into Team Expertise

If you are fortunate to work with a team, including others also means involving appropriate members of your team or the prospect's family, partner, or influencers when necessary to speed up the sales process.

Include *your* team members whenever possible to help:

🕭 Bring additional expertise to the discussion

🕭 Demonstrate the strength or depth within your company

🕭 Match Tribal Type needs more strongly

🕭 Give more opportunity for individual engagement if you are working with a couple or family

One pattern I've noticed is that many advisors don't include the prospect's spouse or partner as early as possible, which can prevent the absent partner from having the same emotional connection to you or the solution.

If you can only talk with one member of a couple, "deputize" the partner in the conversation to be your salesperson to the other partner. Ask them what type of information the absent partner will need to support the next step of the process.

Including and engaging the prospect throughout the entire conversation produces high dividends. They pay closer attention, participate at higher levels, identify a higher perceived value, and will be more inclined to make a buying decision. It keeps Them from sitting back and judging you and your solution.

Action 3: Provide Proof to Support You and Your Solution

Proving yourself—which is denoted in the umbrella over the entire WIIFT system, as shown in Graphic 31-1—shelters you from many common objections and lack of trust issues that can stall your sale. Providing Proof never ends in the selling process; the prospect evaluates your genuineness, expertise, intentions, and value constantly!

Graphic 31-1

Proof also factors in your success in the *Facilitate* step. In fact, it's *the* time to make sure the Proof is enough for that prospect.

During this step, Prove:

- *Who you are.* Every action you take or word you say—or don't take or say—proves something about your character, expertise, and your level of professionalism. This Proof shows throughout the entire conversation and, more importantly, throughout the entire relationship.

- *The value your solution provides.* Providing Proof for your solution is crucial during the Facilitate step. While you are offering an intangible "product," you can still prove its value through examples, testimonials and references, hands-on demos of tools if the prospect desires, and validated third-party research.

The key to Proving is providing the *right* evidence for the person and situation. To help you incorporate relevant Proof information, use your understanding of Tribal Type customs:

- *Commanders* want primary source research, validated proof, metrics, fact sheets, and testimonials that include analysis.

- *Reflectors* need details, guarantees, case studies, conversations with a referral, and an understanding of the whys and hows.

- *Expressers* like personal testimonials, second opinions, references, and a confident advisor.

🌀 *Achievers* want to know the bottom-line output, metrics of outcomes and time considerations, and they want to be able to contact high-profile references.

Continuous Proof is necessary in the *Facilitate* step and throughout the conversation. Can you think of a relationship where, after you've proven yourself once, you never had to again? Not many of us can. Without Proof, it is difficult to move forward in your sales conversation.

Facilitating a Couple Sales Conversation

Facilitating a collaborative and inclusive solution discussion is more complex in couple or family situations. Involving everyone takes preparation and flexibility in the conversation itself. To involve a group, vary the way you *Facilitate* this part of the sales conversation:

🌀 *Ask different types of feedback questions.* Allow the individuals to provide feedback in writing either before or after your meeting.

🌀 *Involve everyone physically and mentally.* Use stories and visual aids and share helpful documents with each person.

🌀 *Facilitate group discovery and clarity.* Ask different people to provide feedback, contribute an idea, use markers or the keyboard, or take notes on a handout.

🌀 *Provide different types of Proof.* This will appeal to the different Tribal Types in the group.

What Do You Do When Your Prospect Isn't a Fit?

What do you do when you realize your prospect isn't qualified or not a fit for your service? What do you do when their feedback indicates they do not see value or think your solution will help with their POWNs?

If you discover you are not a fit, let them know as early as possible to achieve a different type of Win[3]. Everyone wins when you stop trying to fit a round peg into a square hole. *You* win when you are up front and honest, *your company* is saved from a dissatisfied client, and *the prospect* will appreciate your up front approach and honesty.

"Calling it" on a misfit saves everyone a lot of time and energy and allows you to focus on more probable prospect opportunities. Identifying a misfit can also earn you more than a sale—it can earn you a positive reputation and new sales opportunities.

Brian Tegtmeyer of Truly Prosper Financial found just how valuable referring a misfit to another advisor can be, saying, "If you do the right things enough, the right things happen."

Brian, a flat-fee advisor who works with pre-retirees and retirees, conducted an initial conversation with Ryan, a large AUM prospect. Brian used the 4-Point Investigation to uncover Ryan's story and discovered this 40-year-old had over $20 million in assets, businesses that would be bought and sold in the future, and the potential need for complex estate planning. He knew early on that this wasn't going to be the best fit, but he spent an hour with Ryan to make sure he understood his needs so he could make a referral if necessary.

While Brian was tempted to move forward in proposing a solution, he knew Ryan would be better served with another advisor. He told Ryan, "Based on your situations with the businesses, I think someone with business and tax planning expertise for business owners would be able to serve you better."

Ryan was so thankful, telling Brian, "If I can ever refer anyone to you, I absolutely will. I appreciate how honest you are and the time you took with me, knowing I was not a good fit."

If you aren't quite sure if a prospect fits, then circle back to the *Investigate* step or work through your concerns with Stop, Drop, and Roll—the final Action of the *Facilitate* step, which will be introduced in Chapter 34.

CHAPTER 32

Facilitate the Dreaded Fee Discussion

What is put in focus is what is focused on.

—A Nancy Timely Tip

We've reached the fun part—not! Most advisors do not enjoy "talking costs" with prospects.

What a shame! You need to be compensated for the value you provide! And if this part of the conversation or process is awkward for you, it will be for Them as well.

Let's look at how to make talking costs easier for everyone involved.

Action 4: Present Costs Followed by Value

Sharing information about your solution collaboratively might be the easiest part of the *Facilitate* step. But at some point in *Facilitating* your solution, it's time to talk cost. And often this is when the conversation becomes uncomfortable.

It can become uncomfortable when:

🖋 Personal confidence in the value of the solution for the cost is low

🖋 The prospect has not articulated that they see value in the solution—yet

🖋 Expectations around fees and costs haven't been discussed at all, so the advisor has assumptions about what the prospect is willing or able to pay

Working through WIIFT sequentially eliminates these barriers to a productive and value-filled discussion of the costs. This means placing your cost discussion *after* you've collaborated with the prospect and identified the most viable solution connected to WiifTs. Then present the costs (What) followed by value (WiifT). Yes, this is a What to WiifT detail!

Explore the Real Costs of Your Solution

The total costs are not just about money or the fees; the real costs of the prospect securing your service encompass everything: financial costs, time costs, opportunity costs, change costs, relationships costs, and more. Since nonmonetary costs are sometimes the biggest barrier to moving the opportunity forward, you want to set proper expectations for all the costs, leaving no surprises for the prospect after the sale.

Connect the Cost to Value

What is put in focus is what is focused on. The last words spoken or written during any part of the sales conversation hang in the air, like a hologram, for prospects to look at, analyze, and focus on. When the final words are about cost, that's what the prospect is left to focus on. Instead, let those hanging words be about the value—the WiifT.

Connecting cost to value is the same as translating Whats into WiifTs. After all, isn't the cost just another what, or feature, of your solution?

When presented with the costs, the prospect may be thinking, "Is this worth it? Can I afford it? What's in it for me?" Answer the why with the WiifT response to illustrate what they will receive: their POWNs addressed.

The prospect isn't just getting a solution. They're also getting the value or benefits of you and your services: "By working together, you will have the clarity of your total financial picture you've been looking for." "The one-time plan will outline the specific actions for you to take over the next year to get on track with your financial goals."

The language you use when talking cost is important. Terms such as "fee," "price," and "investment" have different connotations. The words you use will resonate differently with different prospects. While "investment" might not be the best in a financial sale, as it may confuse your prospects, helping them translate fees into value that addresses their POWNs makes any cost an investment.

No matter what you call the financial payment for your product or service, delivering the information becomes easier, and perceived value increases, when you connect it to value and how it addresses their POWNs:

*"The fee is 1% of investable assets. For that, you will receive the [white glove, bespoke, customized] comprehensive planning we've discussed, which allows **you** to gain the clarity you want when making your company stock decisions as well as diversifying your investments, so **you** feel less at risk."*

*"You mentioned how important availability is, and that you don't currently have enough access to your advisor. Your annual fee of $15,000 includes the two planned meetings we discussed as well as **you** being able to reach me any other work days for any questions, financial changes, or decisions that pop up."*

Connect the value for them with cost Whats to WiifTs in verbal and written recommendations or proposals.

Traps to Avoid When Talking Cost

When talking costs, our words, actions, and assumptions may send messages we don't intend. These become traps that confuse the value we are trying to communicate.

Words to avoid: Every word you use in your cost discussion sends a message to the prospect. Your words and tone can invite price haggling or demonstrate you lack confidence in your solution. Avoid phrases such as:

- "The fee is usually _____."
- "We kind of use your investable assets as the starting place, and then usually factor in your income level."
- "Is this in the ballpark of what you were expecting?"
- "Our fee is lower than anyone else's." (Unless you aim to be a discount advisor.)

Body language to avoid: Your body language is read carefully by your prospect. Ensure you are not averting your eyes, crossing your arms, positioning your body away from them, or hesitating before talking about the costs.

Assumptions you shouldn't make: Be careful not to impose your personal belief in what someone else should be willing to pay or do when it comes to time or change costs. If you wouldn't invest 2 days to get something done, that doesn't mean the prospect wouldn't. Also, while you often see many details about the prospect's financial situation before discussing fees, don't make assumptions about what they are willing to pay. Many wealthy people always look for huge discounts and many working-class people pay for expertise they don't have.

Don't place low value on your solution: Your personal beliefs about costs significantly impact the cost discussion. If you don't believe your solution is worth the cost, neither will your prospect. To build your belief, identify the Whats to WiifTs before having the prospect conversation. List the Whats on a piece of paper and ask yourself multiple "So Whats?" to identify the value associated with each What. This preparation will boost your confidence and lead to less cost discounting and fewer objections.

* * * * *

This part of the *Facilitate* step can be one of the most rewarding portions of the entire conversation. It's where, given the opportunity, the prospect starts feeling hope, relief, and maybe excitement to work with you!

That is … if you can identify and work through any concerns, challenging questions, or objections they have, which is what we'll review in the next chapters.

CHAPTER 33

Quick Tips to Facilitate the Sharing of Your Solution

In collaborative selling, it's a "we"
dynamic from pre-start to post-finish.

—A Nancy Timely Tip

As you implement the *Facilitate* step, use these quick tips and best practices, from advisors who have completed the Genuine Sales 12-week course. There's also a success story to show the concepts in action.

Quick Tips

- Connect your solution to the value the prospect receives using "Whats to WiifTs."

- Prepare to include your prospect in different ways when discussing your solution. Involve as many senses as possible.

- Leave the WiifT/value as the last image in their mind when sharing cost.

5 Incorporate your prospect's Tribal Type customs into the types of proof and WiifTs you share.

5 For couples or groups, use a variety of inclusion strategies and Proof points to engage and involve everyone.

Advisor's Best Practices and Tips for Facilitating Information Sharing

5 Create a checklist of Whats to WiifTs.

5 Practice the delivery to make it flow easily and avoid clunkiness!

5 Write out a few examples ahead of time.

5 Write down the client's goals and focus on that before the meeting.

5 Investigate more before going to Facilitate by asking better questions.

5 Spend more time in the beginning of Facilitate to set up getting them involved.

5 Prepare.

5 Pause and reiterate.

5 Don't assume the buyer's emotions or what's going through their head.

5 Leverage emotional intelligence to manage seesaw emotions.

5 Prepare for the feedback-question-asking in the Facilitate step.

5 Follow cost with value.

5 As part of the Proof, talk through the intangibles (less stress, less anxiety, an advisor/expert in your corner).

5 Just because the value in excess of fee isn't there for everyone, don't let it impact future prospect conversations.

Success!

Mr. M. had just received a large medical malpractice settlement. I asked him questions about what was important to him and to his family, about his finance knowledge level, how he felt about risk, etc.

I learned through our initial conversation that he was a reflector.

What he wanted was a relationship with a professional that could teach him about finance, help him manage his financial life, and set up his family for success with their goals, which were future weddings for his kids and their first home purchase.

By using the Investigate step, I learned that Mr. M. was very risk-averse. By digging deeper in Investigate, I learned that he was very risk-averse because he didn't know a lot about investing. He shared a desire to be less risk-averse, but he first needed to understand what was happening in his account.

I was able to display to him that I could facilitate growing the funds from his settlement while also educating him about investing, helping him create an investment plan for the future, and giving him peace of mind by making myself accessible.

I think he sincerely appreciated that I didn't judge his very basic questions about finance and responded in a nonjudgmental fashion to even the most basic questions.

Since becoming a client 6 months ago, Mr. M. called last week. He asked to expand his investment portfolio from CDs and Treasuries to include stocks and bonds because he now feels that he has the education and trust with me to further diversify his assets.

–AJ SHOEMAKER, HURLEY CAPITAL

CHAPTER 34

Facilitate, Part II: Work Through Objections

"When solving problems, dig at the roots instead of just hacking at the leaves."

—*Anthony J. D'Angelo*, The College Blue Book

"I object!" While you might hear those words in a courtroom, they usually aren't stated directly, or at all, in a sales conversation. But that doesn't mean you won't be faced with concerns, challenging questions, or outright objections.

Imagine this: You're in a conversation with a prospect and it's going well. You've *Initiated* a positive connection with an agreed-upon objective and engaged in a productive *Investigation* where you discovered their story and specific POWNs. You've *Facilitated* a collaborative discussion of your solution, and they agree your solution will work. You're feeling confident. "But ..." they say. Pay close attention and get ready for them to state a concern or ask a challenging question.

How will you react to the concern or question? Physiologically, we're built to face perceived threats with a fight, flight, or freeze reaction.

🦋 A *Fight* reaction could look like bombarding the prospect with information to talk them into your way of thinking.

🦋 A *Flight* reaction looks like avoiding or minimizing the concern, question, or objection.

🦋 A *Freeze* reaction looks like a long, awkward pause.

None of these reactions advance the sale, trust, collaboration, or relationship.

Your own reaction to the objection as well as the prospect's prior sales "buying" experiences both come into play at this time. The prospect may fear you will ignore their question or concern, and both of you may anticipate a confrontation over fees or another issue.

Can we just avoid all that? Yes, if you first work on your mindset. Concerns and objections in the sales conversation are often nothing more than problems to be solved. When concerns are uncovered, it doesn't have to become an "us or them" situation—at least, not in a WiifT-focused, collaborative selling conversation, where we work *through* objections *with* our prospects.

There is no "handling" or "overcoming" in collaborative selling. Instead, we work together to solve the problem. Even more valuable than solving problems, though, is *resolving* problems.

The difference in solution and *resolution* is significant. While "problem-solution" means identifying an immediate answer or work-around for today, "problem *resolution*" means seeking a long-term solution or permanent fix.

For example, if the fee is the concern, reducing the fee may solve the problem and close the sale today, but what happens in future years? Will the prospect expect the same discount or want deeper ones? That fee reduction is just a solution, whereas, a *resolution* could be a reduced fee for 1 year and an increase to the firm's normal fee in year 2 as their income and earnings rise.

As a long-term *resolution*, this takes into consideration their current situation and accounts for your fee-to-value needs, resulting in a Win^3.

How, then, do you collaborate with them for a mutual, problem-*resolving* outcome? By *Facilitating* them *through* the objection or concern using a strategy you first heard about in your childhood.

Facilitate Action 5: Ask for and Work Through Concerns with Stop, Drop, and Roll

The final Action in the *Facilitate* step of WIIFT is to ask for and work through concerns, challenging questions, and objections (these three items will now be only referenced as "concerns") with a strategy called Stop, Drop, and Roll.

As you work through *Facilitating* the match of your solution to the prospect's POWNs, the prospect will naturally think of concerns. And believe it or not, that's a *good* thing.

After all, we can't work through concerns we don't know about. So, to facilitate the conversation, ask if they have any concerns.

Asking for concerns may seem like we're giving prospects an opportunity to think they should have one. But not asking for them doesn't make them go away; they just remain temporarily buried. The concern will surface eventually—usually when you aren't expecting it. Rather than waiting for that to happen, it's better for all parties to *resolve* the concern quickly, productively, and with a focus on Them.

When a prospect voices a concern, continue collaboration and respond with "Stop, Drop, and Roll."

This represents an important safety tip we learned early in life: if your clothes are on fire, stop, drop to the ground, and roll to extinguish the flames. Though we aren't literally on fire when we hear a concern, our body reacts to a perceived threat in the same way, and a fight, flight, or freeze response kicks in!

Graphic 34-1

I promise I will not suggest you drop and roll on the ground though a creative group in Australia sent me a video of them doing it just for fun! The collaborative selling Stop, Drop, and Roll, Graphic 34-1, is a mental and verbal strategy for working *through* concerns. Let's dig in below to review how we apply this strategy.

When a concern is raised, use this strategy for collaborative problem-solving:

- *Stop* what you are doing, saying, and thinking to pay attention to the prospect. Let them completely finish what they are saying. Make eye contact, listen to their words and tone, and observe their body language. This pause allows you to take a breath or two and engage your mind before your mouth.

- *Drop* your defenses, agenda, assumptions, emotions, and ego before saying anything. Take another breath.

- *Roll* forward or backward in WIIFT by working as a problem resolver with Them using the 3 A's as your guide: Acknowledge the objection, Ask clarifying questions, and Answer collaboratively.

CHAPTER 35

The 3 A's to Roll Through Concerns and Objections

There can be multiple root causes for nearly any concern, challenging question, or objection.

—A Nancy Timely Tip

Acknowledge, Ask, & Answer

Ready to learn about the 3 A's? These are your guide to what to say and DO when you hear a concern, challenging question, or objection.

Acknowledge the Concern

After a concern is voiced, and you have Stopped and Dropped, the first words *you* say are to *Acknowledge* Them. State an *Acknowledge* phrase followed by a short paraphrase of their concern to let the prospect know that you heard them and will not fight, freeze, or flee from the concern.

Acknowledgment sounds like this:

🖋 "I understand that the timing of starting doesn't work for you."

🖋 "What I hear you saying is that you have questions about my experience in this area."

Notice that *Acknowledgment* phrases focus on *hearing* their concern or objection, not *agreeing* with them. Agreeing with their concern can seem condescending, as if you are pacifying them or faking it.

You can begin your *Acknowledgment* in many ways. To avoid sounding scripted, use phrases that are comfortable for you and that resonate with your prospect's Tribal Type, such as:

🖋 "I appreciate knowing or hearing _____."

🖋 "Thank you for sharing that _____."

🖋 "What I hear you saying is _____."

🖋 "Uh-huh, or Okay, _____."

🖋 "I can understand that _____."

🖋 "It sounds like _____."

🖋 "If I understand you correctly, _____."

🖋 "Okay, you wonder _____."

A word of caution: Be careful that your *Acknowledgment* does not "name" their emotion. Avoid phrases like "I understand your *frustration*" or "I hear that you are *afraid* that _____." If they haven't named their emotion, neither should you. If you name the wrong emotion, you create a new concern.

If you tell the prospect you understand they are afraid, confused, or frustrated, and that is not their emotion, they might then want to address their emotions instead of the real concern. Instead, say "I understand that you are saying _____," or "I hear that you _____," and then paraphrase the concern.

If you followed the 3 A's framework "by the book," you would immediately follow *Acknowledging* their concerns with *Asking* clarifying questions. But after years of listening to advisor phone sales conversations, I noticed a pattern that some advisors add naturally that makes a big difference.

The Segue

It's the segue: the connector between *Acknowledge* and *Ask*. It powerfully reduces the prospect's potential apprehension about the *Acknowledgement* being a setup to being "sold to" with a premature *Answer.*

A segue has many benefits.

🔊 Shares your intention and lessens their fight/flight response

🔊 Gains permission to ask for more information

🔊 Demonstrates you are still collaborating

🔊 Sets the stage for working through the objection together

A segue guides the prospect forward into a continued collaborative conversation.

🔊 "Your question about the fees is interesting. (Pause.) And because there are so many directions we can go with this question, is it okay if I first ask you a few questions?"

✒ "I appreciate you letting me know that your current advisor takes care of your parents as part of their service to you. (Pause.) Let's discuss that further, please. I'd like to ask a couple of questions to help me better understand this."

Ask Clarifying Questions

After *Acknowledging* that you hear the prospect, segue as explained, and then *Ask* questions to clarify that you have heard the root concern. This doesn't slow down the problem-solving; in fact, surfacing additional information may actually speed up the process of resolution. As American author and magazine editor Dorothea Brande said, "A problem clearly stated is a problem half solved."

Any concern can have multiple root causes. And if you *Answer* and share information from the first words they stated, you may be wasting everyone's time. Because often the first concern stated isn't the real one. It's the easy one.

For example, the root causes of a prospect objecting to you managing all their assets could include lack of full trust, a desire to preserve an existing financial relationship, calculations that this will increase their fee, a desire to personally control some assets for other pursuits, and more.

That's why we need to Stop and *Ask* open-ended questions to clarify the concern and ensure we address it with a relevant *Answer*. Seeking this clarity prevents you from wasting time and energy on solving the wrong problem.

The first clarifying question should be indirect, non-defensive, and designed to seek understanding and more information. Start with a "soft" question to ensure the prospect's emotions are not out of proportion with the concern.

Gaps in information often create concerns. As prospects clarify the concern, they often talk themselves through it, removing the concern before it becomes necessary for you to offer fee discounting, concessions, or changes to the service or terms.

Segue from your *Acknowledgment* to the *Ask* with phrases such as these:

- "So that I can determine what can be done, _____? There are a few questions to explore."

- "Let's see how we might look at this together. May I ask a couple of questions to better understand?"

- "Let's explore that further. I have a couple of questions."

- "I'd like to better understand this. Is it okay to ask a few more questions?"

Then pause to give their brain and body a chance to reduce its fight-or-flight response, and *Ask* questions or phrases that request more information, like the thought-starters that follow:

- "What makes the _____ challenging for you?"

- "Help me understand more about your feelings or thoughts that _____."

- "How do you see this affecting what we've discussed?"

- "Please tell me more ..."

- "How did that come to mind?"

- "What's prompting that question (or concern)?"

Listen to their response, then paraphrase and, if necessary, ask another clarifying question.

A caution about your clarifying questions: Be aware that asking *why* may cause a defensive reaction. Though we need to understand where the objection is coming from, a *why* question can put the person on the defense and make it harder for us to collaborate with Them. Instead, start with: "How does _____?" or "What makes _____?"

Two to three follow-up questions may be needed to understand the real concern. Don't rush this part of the conversation!

Answer Collaboratively

After the prospect clarifies their concern, you determine which way to Roll in WIIFT—back to the *Investigate* step to further explore POWNs with additional questions or to the earlier Actions in the *Facilitate* step to discuss more WiifTs. You may also find you have addressed the concern through clarifying questions and can simply Roll forward to *Then Consolidate*.

Since a collaborative approach to concerns might be a new approach—and a welcome one—for your prospect, set a collaborative intention by letting the prospect know that you want to work *with* Them to identify the best resolution. Give Them hope that their concerns can be resolved with a start to collaborative *Answers* like these:

- "I can see how this is a concern for you. There are several ways we can address this. Would you like to see what we can do to explore additional options?"

- "Thank you for explaining further. What I recommended may not fit as well as I thought with the initial information I had. With the new details you shared, we can look at other options that may suit your needs better."

As you *Answer*, use the Whats to WiifT format discussed in Chapter 30 to connect the details to the What's in it for Them. In some cases, your *Answer* may be a clear-cut explanation of certain details or information. At other times, you might not have one straightforward *Answer*, either because several options are viable or because a resolution is not available. In these situations, your *Answer* should be a collaborative discussion with Them to identify alternatives, change the scope of the solution, or declare you're not a fit.

That's how Stop, Drop, and Roll, again shown in Graphic 35-1, keeps the conversation collaborative. It's a strategy we can employ at any point in the conversation when a concern is stated, not just during the *Facilitate* step.

Stop Drop Roll™

Stop	Drop	Roll
Pause & Listen	Defenses, Assumptions, Agendas, & Emotions	Acknowledge, Ask, & Answer

Graphic 35-1

Your approach to any concern is going to either move you through it collaboratively or create a barrier that you will need to climb over at some point. Using Stop, Drop, and Roll with *Acknowledge, Ask*, and *Answer* removes all barriers and advances you through the rest of the WIIFT conversation.

TIMELY TIP

To *Facilitate* through a concern *when working with a couple or group*, adjust the Stop, Drop, and Roll process. Stop, then Drop the agenda, ego, and assumptions. Roll with an *Acknowledgment* of the objection, and then *Ask* your clarifying question, first to the person stating the concern and then to the others if necessary. They may resolve the concern among themselves. If not, continue to *Ask* and *Answer* as appropriate. Then Roll forward to the rest of the conversation.

Stop, Drop, and Roll looks easy enough, doesn't it? And it can be, especially when you prepare yourself to implement it effectively by learning about the nuances of *Facilitate* in the next chapter.

CHAPTER 36

The Nuances for Working through Concerns

Working with the logical and emotional influences of the prospect is important throughout the sales process— and especially when the prospect has concerns.

—A Nancy Timely Tip

Stop, Drop, and Roll is an effective strategy for not only "addressing" but also "working through" concerns, challenging questions, and outright objections from your prospects. And like all good best practices, you can increase your effectiveness by understanding the nuances described in this chapter.

Prepare to Work through Concerns

Preparation is important for every part of the conversation, especially when it comes to getting in front of concerns! The QPT (Graphic

44–1 in chapter 44) includes a specific section for you to do just that. This preparation (the habit you will grow to love when you consistently do it for the entire conversation) helps you to remain collaborative at the right moment in the conversation and sales process.

To prepare to address concerns:

- Identify and list probable concerns, challenging questions, or objections that might be raised in this specific conversation

- Identify the potential root causes for the concern to help guide the next items

- Make note of potential open-ended clarifying questions to ask if a concern or question is raised

- Plan to get in front of the concern by discussing potential concerns early in the conversation

- Identify additional *Investigate* questions you might ask to discover information before it becomes a concern or obstacle

- Prepare proof or validation materials to use before a concern surfaces or when working through a stated concern

In addition to preparing for specific conversations, you can prepare for the most common concerns or questions raised in your sales conversations. Each time you hear a concern, make note of it, then:

- Research information such as proof points, examples of alternatives, pricing options, and policies that may help you work through the concern in different situations and with different prospects. For example, if the concern is about the fee, research how other firms with service models like yours calculate the fee.

- Talk with others in your firm or industry who may hear the same concerns. Ask them how they work through it. Ask them for information about the types of proof they use and resolutions they have found work well. This information may save you time and effort.

🖋 Practice your responses to each concern. In our fee example, to practice, state your fee and how it is calculated and connect the solution to various WiifTs.

🖋 When the fee concern is next raised, take a breath or two and mentally review this pre-work. Then move forward in implementing the 3 A's, providing supporting data to work through the objection or question on cost.

Building your knowledge base for common concerns allows you to be a better problem *resolver* the next time you hear that specific concern.

Tap into Emotions That Hinder Concern Resolution

Many emotions are involved during the entire sales process—excitement, anticipation, fear, frustration, confidence, disappointment, and irritation, to name a few. These emotions can escalate when a concern is voiced. In fact, these emotions—and how we handle them—may hinder our ability to work through concerns.

Working with the prospect's logical *and* emotional responses is important throughout the sales process—especially when the prospect has concerns. Sometimes working with emotions is an obstacle in itself.

You may have been taught that you should "mirror" or match the prospect's emotions throughout the sales process. But do you really want to match anger with anger, frustration with more frustration, or irritation with irritation?

Probably not. Matching those emotions would hurt your ability to work through the concern. What often works is *adjusting your level of intensity.*

Communicate with Intensity

Many communication "misses" and escalated objections are caused by a mismatch of *intensity*, which is one aspect of emotions. The following real-life example highlights a mismatch:

Prospect, with a medium tone and volume: You just gave me the wrong product after a long wait. I'd like a refund.

Seller, very calmly: Yes, there was an error in fulfillment. What would you like us to do?

Prospect, louder and more anxiously: I would like you to take back this product and give me a refund like I asked.

Seller, very calmly with a lower voice: Well, we can do that, and the refund will take 30 days to process through your account.

Prospect, incredulous and loud: I don't think *you* get this. I have already paid and waited 30 minutes, and then you gave me the wrong item. I want an immediate refund.

The extremely calm Seller: I'm sorry to hear that. Our policy is to issue a refund in 30 days.

Prospect, irritated and increasingly frustrated: Well that doesn't make sense!

Why was the prospect getting more frustrated? The seller was saying some of the right things—in a very calm and low-key way that came off as patronizing. This calmness caused the prospect to escalate her emotional reaction and intensity because she didn't think the seller was "getting it." She became more emotional to try to communicate the degree of her frustration.

The seller kept missing my signals of irritation and despair (yes, I was the irritated prospect). What I needed to know was that he understood that the gift I was expecting to give my husband for his birthday wasn't available, and I didn't know what to do. I needed empathy and understanding, not a refund in the mail 30 days later.

The disconnection in intensity led to misunderstanding, less engagement, and loss of business (I didn't go into that store again for almost 8 years). He wasn't really *hearing* me. Yes, he listened to my words, but he wasn't getting the intensity and emotions that told the real story and the importance of the purchase.

Had the advisor been more animated and emphasized his concern with an increase in tone and energy, we might have headed in a more mutually agreeable direction. I would have felt that he cared and that I mattered.

What does this information on intensity mean for all of us? When we try to understand and connect with the person while also paying attention to and adjusting to match their intensity, their level of satisfaction and loyalty will increase even if we can't *resolve* the concern. You might need to adjust up or down; getting to the right level is what matters.

No, we don't need to match the *same* level of intensity, but we need to increase our intensity enough to show that we "get it," or rather, get them! This may mean becoming more animated, making more direct eye contact, and raising the pitch in our voice a bit. It may also mean becoming less of all these.

Sometimes I see advisors get more intense and animated when the prospect begins to back off or seems uninterested, thinking that intensity will generate a higher level of interest. This mismatch of intensity usually backfires, accelerates distrust, and causes the prospect to dismiss the discussion as superficial.

One last time: We need to *adjust our intensity level*, not get emotional with Them.

Demonstrate Empathy

While intensity is important to not get drug into potentially unhealthy emotions, empathy is important!

More specifically, 2 kinds of empathy:[9]

---

[9] Kendra Cherry, "What Is Empathy?" Very Well Mind, Updated on February 22, 2023, https://www.verywellmind.com/what-is-empathy-2795562.

🔥 Affective empathy: the ability to respond to other people's emotions appropriately.

🔥 Cognitive empathy: the ability to understand someone's response to a situation.

Each of these can be a challenge if you disagree or don't "get" their concern. Or maybe you've heard it so many times and think it's silly or unnecessary.

During the discussion of concerns, both affective and cognitive empathy are important. By demonstrating empathy to the prospective client, they feel heard and seen.

The entire Stop, Drop, and Roll framework with *Acknowledge, Ask,* and *Answer* sets up an empathetic approach to addressing the concern. Yet your delivery, tone, pace, and eye contact during this part of the conversation is important.

That's why Stop and Drop first allows your primal reactions to abate and your heart and head deliver the Roll's 3 A's with empathy.

Skip the "Buts" That Hinder Collaboration

A single word can ignite a defensive emotional reaction. If your *Acknowledgment* statement is followed by "but" or "however," that one word can negate your acknowledgment and send the message "I hear you, and now I'm going to tell you why you are wrong." It lowers trust and collaboration and creates a fight-or-flight response from the prospect.

"But" or "however" in a sentence contradicts the first part of your *Acknowledgment.* The word "but" is often simply inserted as a connector between two statements, not as a contradictor. However, your prospects don't have time to figure out which part of the statement is the real message, so they will most likely focus on the last part of what you say. We don't want to shut down our collaborative selling approach with just one word. Consider these examples:

🖋 "It sounds like the fee is a concern for you, **but** let me tell you a story about why we have our fees structured like this."

🖋 "I appreciate you asking that question, **but** that's an industry standard."

🖋 "I'm sorry you don't like the answer, **but** that's all I can offer."

The big question then is ... how do we *Acknowledge* we hear them and segue into a response or question? There are two simple approaches:

🖋 End your *Acknowledgment* with a pause (or use a period in writing). Then, after the pause, start the second sentence with a segue into your clarifying question.

🖋 Use the word "and" to connect the *Acknowledgment* with the segue that follows.

Using these two approaches to skipping the "buts," the above examples could be restated like this:

🖋 "It sounds like the fee is a concern for you. (**pause**) I may have missed something as we talked. Let's explore this further together."

🖋 "I appreciate you asking the question, **and** there are different ways for us to address that. Let's look at how by unpacking that question further."

🖋 "I'm sorry you don't like the answer, **and** it would be helpful for us to discuss that further. Can I ask a couple of questions?"

The use of "but" as a connector is a bad habit, one that might jeopardize your success in working through the prospect's concern. "Skipping the buts" takes effort, and it is well worth that effort. The payoff is a clear message from you and a conversation that continues.

On the other hand, when the prospect says "but," listen up! They may be using "but" to state a concern or to ask a question. When you hear a "but," in this context use Stop, Drop, and Roll to work through the concern that follows it.

Strategies to Work through Concerns with the Tribal Types

Have you ever noticed how many ways different prospects will react when concerns surface? A prospect's Tribal Type customs influence them strongly when they feel they are under pressure. Their unique information needs, their collaboration preferences, and their fears influence how they approach a concern. The good news is that you can adjust your Stop, Drop, and Roll delivery for each Tribe.

Achievers are decisive and want to get things done. They may think that concerns are time-wasters. You may find that they express concerns before hearing all the information, get frustrated when a concern isn't answered immediately, don't raise concerns at times because they don't want to slow down the progress, or push for an answer without exploring options.

To work through concerns with Achievers, use these strategies:

- Let them know that concerns will be addressed quickly.
- Ask for their ideas on possible solutions to the concern.
- Clarify what the real concern is and discuss its impact on results and time frame.

Commanders will want the solution to be "right." They will analyze the solution from all angles, ask a lot of "why" questions, willingly express their concern or question when asked, may ask for time to think, and form firm opinions.

To work through concerns with Commanders, use these strategies:

- Approach your clarifying questions in a logical, factual way.
- Ask for their opinions and suggestions for resolving the concern.
- Let the solution be their idea.

Reflectors do not want to rush or confront. They may not state their concerns unless they are asked. You may find that they avoid potential conflict, agree easily even if it is to their disadvantage, prefer time to consider options, and are not comfortable being put on the spot.

To work through concerns with Reflectors, use these strategies:

- *Acknowledge* their concerns with feeling and empathy.

- Reassure them (through body language and words) that their concerns are valid and will be addressed.

- Discuss their fears and the potential risks of the solution.

Expressers don't like conflict or confrontation. They don't want to hurt your feelings—even though they may have concerns. They may agree with you and go along with a commitment ... for now. Then you may find that they stall when it comes to taking action, don't return your phone calls or messages, become less open with information, or involve others later rather than sooner.

To work through concerns with Expressers, use these strategies:

- Ask for questions or concerns assertively.

- Assure them you want to work through any potential concerns with Them and that everyone can succeed and win.

- Demonstrate (through body language and words) the desire to collaborate.

- Use "feeling" words and "who" questions: "What types of questions do you feel others might have about this?" "Who else should be involved in giving feedback on what we've recommended?"

Subtle changes in how you *Acknowledge, Ask*, and *Answer* with each Tribal Type make a huge difference in their willingness to work with you.

Traps to Avoid When Faced with Concerns

While Stop, Drop, and Roll helps you work through concerns, you should be aware of traps and blind spots that will diminish your effectiveness.

Past Experience Bias

Your past relationship and experiences with your prospect may shape your reaction to their concerns. You may think, "Here we go again," or "They always do this."

Assumptions

Avoid making assumptions about their concerns or where the conversation is going. Assumptions will keep you from listening and clarifying the concern and may lead you to make mistakes. You may have heard the concern hundreds, if not thousands, of times, but it's your prospect's first time, and they need you to work them through it without shortcutting the process. Take the time to listen to and clarify their concerns.

Hasty Responses

If you try to resolve the situation quickly, you may prematurely make commitments you don't want to keep later, such as discounting fees or expanding the scope of services. So, when they state their concern, remember to Stop, take a breath if you need to, and then *Acknowledge.*

Negative Mindsets

Facilitating through a concern successfully begins with how you think about it. The concepts of "concern" and "negotiation" often have negative connotations. You might associate these concepts with words like "manipulation," "confrontation," or "winners and losers." These associations do not lead to the mindset needed for collaborative problem resolution.

Instead of these negative thoughts, think of objections as an *opportunity* to achieve the following:

 Collaborate with your prospect as a problem resolver.

 Strengthen your connection with the prospect as you focus on their ideas, concerns, and feelings.

 Educate yourself and the prospect. Perhaps we need to learn something from them because we didn't ask or they didn't share specific details earlier. Or perhaps the prospect needs to learn more about the solution, proof, or details.

 Show expertise. Our ability to work through objections collaboratively by sharing examples, ideas, and suggestions shows our flexibility, knowledge, and experience.

Converting concerns, challenging questions, and objections into opportunities for collaborative problem *resolution* takes skill and discipline, achieved through preparation and practice. You may need to retrain your brain to respond differently than you naturally would.

You'll increase your probability of success when you work through concerns with a collaborative, opportunity-focused mindset.

CHAPTER 37

Quick Tips and Best Practices to Work Effectively Through Concerns

As you implement the *Facilitate* step, use these quick tips and best practices, from advisors who have completed the Genuine Sales 12-week course. There's also a success story to show the concepts in action.

Quick Tips

- Stop, Drop, and Roll when you hear a concern, challenging question, or objection.

- *Acknowledge* the prospect's objection, segue into an Ask for clarification, and then Answer appropriately.

- Show, by your level of intensity, that you understand their concern, that you are listening, and that you really hear Them.

- Skip the "buts" and "howevers" after you *Acknowledge* their concern.

- Adjust the delivery of Stop, Drop, and Roll to the Tribal Types' customs.

🦚 Develop the mindset that you add more value to the prospect's experience by viewing the objection as an opportunity to be an effective problem *resolver.*

Advisor's Best Practices and Tips for Working Through Concerns

🦚 Uncover the real source of the objection and not the surface-level objection.

🦚 When a prospect voices a concern, pause and silently count to 8 before saying anything. Use this pause to regroup mentally when objections arise.

🦚 Don't say "but" or "however" after *Acknowledging* a concern.

🦚 Make a list of recent or most common objections and prepare good responses. Have proof to back up answers.

🦚 Prepare responses to potential objections regarding ongoing fees.

🦚 Be ready and plan to go through the Stop, Drop, and Roll process with a prospective client. Treat it as part of the process instead of allowing yourself to be caught off guard.

🦚 Show appreciation for them speaking their mind and then ask them to expand more on their thoughts.

🦚 Paraphrase when *Acknowledging* and *Asking.*

🦚 Prepare a couple of universal *Acknowledgments* and segues to avoid getting overwhelmed by too many options.

🦚 Tie your answers to objections back to their POWNs.

🦚 Ask open-ended questions when encountering an objection. Fully understand a client's perspective.

🦚 Remember to roll back and *Investigate* further when needed.

🦚 Don't overexplain.

Success!

I heard an objection from an existing client, who is an Expresser. She wanted to state and address the objection via text message, but I asked for a phone call. I was able to use the Stop, Drop, and Roll tool to walk through the objection with the client over the phone, which helped me keep the business and gain another account. The framework of Stop, Drop, and Roll helped me not panic during her objections, understand her Tribal Type, and be more comfortable in that conversation than I normally would be.

–COLLIN MASCAGNI, MASCAGNI WEALTH MANAGEMENT

CHAPTER 38

Then Consolidate: Close Every Conversation with Purpose

"Decisions determine destiny."

—Frederick Speakman, author

The end is near! The end of your conversation, that is. After all the hard work collaborating with your prospect through the WIIFT steps, it would be a shame to not wrap up the conversation as purposefully as you began it. Your last step, *Then Consolidate*, guides you to a productive conversation closure—and a conversion.

A productive conversation ends with them deciding or committing to *do* something. If you don't guide them to a next step at the end of the conversation, all the talk about their POWNs is for naught, as a lack of action prolongs the sales cycle and frustrates the prospect, you, and everyone on your team.

Too many advisors work hard to build the relationship, identify the POWNs, demonstrate their services' value, and then wait …

follow up with the prospect, wait … follow up with the prospect again, and then wait some more. What they don't do is *ask* for a decision or commitment to advance or make the sale.

When I ask advisors, "What keeps you from working with more clients?" I often hear, "The prospects don't make timely decisions," or "I thought it went well, and then they ghosted me." Yet, when I ask prospects why they didn't move forward, their response is often, "They never asked me!"

Then Consolidate is your guide to advancing or making the sale by asking for and securing the decision or commitment. It also helps you set the right expectations by identifying next steps, strengthening the relationship, and closing the conversation.

Why "consolidate" instead of "close"? Closing sales is typically an outcome—securing the buy decision. But *Then Consolidate* is more; it's the step that unites all the previous steps to easily advance or make the sale.

Consolidating is important because, without a decision to work with you, a Win[3] may not be achieved: the prospect never receives the value of your service, you don't get to use your knowledge to help, and your firm loses a potential client and revenue.

 The Then Consolidate Step Overview

 Objectives

- ✓ Assist with decision making
- ✓ Agree on next steps
- ✓ Strengthen the relationship
- ✓ Close the conversation

 Actions/How-tos

1. Complete a Decision Readiness check
2. Confirm the value your solution will provide
3. Ask for a decision or commitment to action
4. Identify the next steps with specifics
5. Close the conversation

Know What You Are Closing

Not every sales conversation ends with a final decision to work together; you may still need multiple conversations and a series of decisions before reaching that point. That's why your Preparation, the focus of the *Wait* step introduced in Chapters 15 to 19, *begins* with identifying the objective or desired outcome for the conversation.

Clarifying your desired outcome ensures you have the best conversation to reach the successful outcome you seek. Typically, desired sales conversation outcomes include:

⑨ Getting the yes or securing the conversion.

⑨ Fact-finding to surface specific information about POWNs and qualify the prospect for fit.

⑨ A strong relationship built by collaborating throughout the entire process.

⑨ Achieving an introduction to someone else—client referrals to the prospect's spouse, friends, family, or other groups or influencers.

I've always been amazed at how little preparation is put into ending a sales conversation and how many sales are stalled or lost because of it. Knowing what you want or need to happen identifies your objective for the conversation. It's the start of successfully completing WIIFT and conversion.

We started the conversation in *Initiate* with a 3-Step Start, so it's only fitting to wrap up the WIIFT conversation with a 3-Step Finish, shown in Graphic 38-1: the first 3 Actions in *Then Consolidate*.

Graphic 38-1

Asking for a decision may feel like you are about to jump off a cliff. Well, it shouldn't be that way! We need to strap on the parachute first. And that's what the 3-Step Finish, the anchor for *Then Consolidate*, does. It guides us to a safe landing.

To keep us from aggressively "going for the ask" or tentatively "kind of" asking, the 3-Step Finish guides us to first evaluate whether the prospect is ready or not with a check-in.

CHAPTER 39

Then Consolidate:
The 3-Step Finish

The easiest and most efficient way to close or advance more sales is to complete the earlier steps of WIIFT® and then ask the prospect to make a decision or commitment.

—A Nancy Timely Tip

Check
for decision
readiness

Action 1: Complete a Decision Readiness Check

Consolidating begins with identifying whether your prospect is ready to make a decision or commitment. Rather than a "trial close," as it's sometimes called, I think of it as a readiness check because it's an opportunity for both you and them to determine if they are ready to move forward or if something is holding them back. In WIIFT, we don't ask until we know the prospect is ready. This decision readiness check is your opportunity to test the proverbial waters before asking for a decision, ensuring you have accomplished what you both needed.

It also keeps you from overselling and possibly losing the sale.

Fortunately, the readiness check often leads the prospect to make the decision then and there.

If they answer Readiness Questions positively but don't share a decision, then the next 2 Actions—Confirm and Ask—are put into play.

If you find they are not ready, you may need to move back to a previous step in the WIIFT system.

How do you check readiness? By paying attention to the prospect's clues:

- Body language signals
- Words and sounds
- Readiness Question responses

Look for Body Language Signals

Paying attention to the prospect's communication signals is important throughout the entire conversation, and perhaps even more so at the end. If you meet with your prospects face-to-face or virtually, observing the clues they send with their bodies gives you some insight into their state of readiness.

Positive body language signals include more relaxed movements, making eye contact with you, leaning toward you, and smiling. Prospects also send clues such as collecting their papers, looking at their phone or clock, making impatient body movements, making eye contact with fellow prospects, standing up, or closing their laptop to indicate they want the conversation to end.

Our dilemma in reading body language is that we don't know if they want to end the conversation because they have what they need and are ready to move forward in the sale, because they have made a "no" decision, or because they have just run out of time. We need to increase our understanding of our visual check-in with verbal clues.

TIMELY TIP

Body language clues can be misread. A head nodding yes doesn't mean the prospect is agreeing with you: it means they are agreeing with what they are thinking. In some cultures, a nod is simply a way of showing respect and communicating that they hear you.

Listen for Readiness Words and Sounds

If you are one of the millions of advisors who never see your prospect, visual messages are nonexistent. That's why words and other sounds are valuable clues for identifying readiness. And if you are in the same room with your prospect, observing both visual cues and words and sounds helps you interpret their readiness more accurately.

Prospects send clues about their readiness with the words they use. They may talk as if they are already working with you. These phrases and questions indicate their readiness to commit to working with you:

- "When we start this ..."
- "Will you be helping us _____?"
- "It looks like we could start on this ..."
- "How do your fees get paid?"
- "This is so much more than we get from our current advisor."

What prospects say is a clue to their readiness to move forward. It isn't a complete signal, which is why you must also observe how they communicate at this point of the conversation:

🌀 *Pauses and hesitations in their speech* may indicate unstated concerns or questions.

🌀 *An increase in their pace of speech* could signal that they are ready to move forward and would like you to move things along. Or it could mean that they want to end the conversation because they have made a "no" decision.

🌀 *The confidence in their voice* and tone is a gauge of their certainty in making a decision.

🌀 *Background noises*, such as shuffling papers or keyboard clicking, are clues that may indicate they are distracted and no longer paying attention, and that they need the conversation to end.

We can use these signals to help us determine readiness. Yet, we still don't know if the words and sounds mean they are *really* ready unless we *ask* Them.

Ask Readiness Questions and Listen to the Responses

By matching the clues of body language and the prospect's words and sounds with a Readiness Question, you confirm what you are observing. Responses to Readiness Questions clearly identify where prospects are in their thoughts—and in the decision process as well. Readiness Questions also check for any final objections or concerns.

Here are some thought-starters for Readiness Questions:

🌀 "Have we covered all the information you need to make a decision or move forward?"

🌀 "How does what we've discussed sound to you?"

🌀 "How do you feel about the process we have reviewed?"

🌀 "Do you feel like you have a solution to the issue we first discussed?"

🌀 "What concerns do you have about this solution or about me or my company?"

⚡ "After our conversation, are you feeling better about the issue you were concerned about?"

⚡ "Have we covered everything that was on your mind?"

⚡ "How does that match up with what you were considering?"

⚡ "What obstacles do you see in implementing this?"

⚡ "What else do you need to know to make the best decision?"

⚡ "Are there any final open items we need to cover?"

⚡ "What are your feelings or thoughts about the solution we've presented?"

⚡ "How does our service line up with your expectations?"

⚡ "What are your next actions in making a decision?"

⚡ "Does what we've talked about today align with your goal of _____?"

⚡ "Have we provided all the details you need to know?"

Notice that I've listed both closed- and open-ended questions. The open-ended Readiness Questions provide the prospect with the opportunity to tell you more about the *why* of their level of readiness. Closed-ended Readiness Questions are also helpful because we need to start hearing yes or no—and so does the prospect. When prospects hear themselves say yes, they often talk themselves into the decision and ask *you* for the next step in buying at this point. It's powerful persuasion.

With closed-ended Readiness Questions, be ready to ask a follow-up question based on their response. If you receive a positive response, then move to the next Action in *Then Consolidate*. If you hear a negative response, move back a step or two in WIIFT. You may need to *Investigate* further or refocus the prospect on your solution's value and work through additional concerns in *Facilitate*. That's okay. Revisiting previous WIIFT steps helps you move forward when the time is right.

Readiness Questions are aimed at keeping the conversation collaborative, building *your* confidence in asking for the decision, and ensuring you aren't overselling.

Action 2: Confirm the Value Your Solution Will Provide

Positive responses to the decision readiness check move you into the decision arena. Segue into the decision question by first recapping their POWNs and confirming the value of your solution to provide one last reminder of WiifT and show them why they should make a decision now.

Confirming value before the Ask keeps you from sounding random or disjointed. "Do you want to move to scheduling our first meeting?" or "Ready to sign the agreement?" without a segue can make the prospect feel defensive. Instead, segue into the Ask by Confirming the value of your solution.

Consider these examples:

- "Chris, as we reviewed, in working together we'll organize all your accounts so you have a clear picture of your finances and can feel more confident in Prem leaving her job after the baby is born."

- "You'll be able to confidently declare your retirement date after we complete the first 3 meetings to create your plan."

In these 2 examples, the real value that they receive is:

- Clear data to make a decision on living on one income
- Confidence in setting a retirement date

Confirming the value reminds prospects of what they will really receive—a solution that addresses their POWNs. The perceived value of your solution increases when you confirm the WiifTs—and so does the likelihood that they will make a positive decision.

You can resolve many concerns, fears, and stalls as you remind prospects one final time What's in it for Them. This is an effective setup in asking for the decision or commitment.

After confirming value with strong WiifTs and outcomes, *pause* for 1 to 3 seconds, then move on to Action 3.

Action 3: Ask for a Decision or Commitment to Action

Now you have the perfect segue into the Ask. Using the same examples above, let's segue into the Ask:

"Chris, as we reviewed, in working together we'll organize all your accounts so you have a clear picture of your finances and can feel more confident in Prem leaving her job after the baby is born. Would you like to see the official agreement?"

"You'll be able to confidently declare your specific retirement date after we complete the first 3 meetings to create your plan. Should we schedule the first of these meetings today?"

The easiest and most efficient way to close or advance more sales is to complete the earlier steps of WIIFT and then *ask* the prospect to make a decision or commitment.

Let's look at some Decision Question thought-starters:

- "Are you ready to move forward?"
- "Would you like to schedule our discovery call?"
- "Are you ready to schedule a _____ meeting?"
- "Are you ready to sign the agreement?"
- "Are you ready for us to send you the Advisory Agreement?"
- "Can we schedule the next meeting to review our planning process in more detail now?"
- "Would you like me to get the paperwork started?"
- "When would you like for this process to begin?"
- "Are there any other items to discuss before we send over the agreement? Who will be the signer?"
- "Would you like to move forward in working together?"

A decision is what is needed. A no response is better than no answer, because then you can move on to more probable opportunities. If you get a yes, you've just converted a new client!

To confidently and successfully ask for a decision, use these strategies:

- *Be specific.* Clearly ask for a specific decision or action, such as "Are you ready to move forward?" or "Can we initiate the paperwork today?"
- *Be assertive in asking for ONE decision.* Asking a complex question such as "Are you ready to make the next step, or do you need more information?" complicates the situation and indicates insecurity.

So does "Would you like to schedule the onboarding meeting, or do you want more time to decide?"

- *Pause after asking* the decision question and wait for them to respond. Do not minimize the importance of making a decision or try to rush them.

- *Use a confident tone.* Their responses to your Readiness Questions should have removed your fear of a negative response. Keep your voice steady.

- Make eye contact when you ask.

- *Adapt your question* to their Tribal Type.

Securing this decision verbally is important. If the prospect doesn't specifically answer, then you are moving forward on assumptions— and you know what happens when you assume, don't you? You might be wrong and set yourself up for disaster.

This lesson was reinforced as I sat behind the exit row on an airplane. Before the plane departed, the flight attendant approached the passengers in the exit rows to explain their role in case of an emergency. She then asked them if they were willing to help others in an emergency. All four passengers nodded their head in agreement, but the attendant said, "I need you to verbally tell me yes or no."

As I watched this situation, I thought, "That's what's often missing in converting opportunities. We pay attention to body language and make assumptions. But if we don't have a verbal commitment or agreement, we might be setting ourselves up for a disaster later."

Advisors often neglect to ask prospects to do anything. Instead, the advisor often says, "This was a lot of information, and you probably need time to go home and think about it. I'll follow up with you next week if that's okay." Or they might say, "I'll send you the agreement to look over. Let me know if you have any questions." Really? Those are passive next steps on their part.

In cases like these, the prospects have committed to nothing! You have told them what you are doing, and it didn't help you assess their commitment to moving forward. So, you've most likely started the chase and follow-up fun.

Your prospects need you to confidently ask them to make a verbal commitment to an action or a decision. Whether the decision is an approval or acceptance, a commitment to a next meeting, an introduction to someone else, a commitment to send specific statements, documents, or information, or a commitment to review information, we need them to say yes.

CHAPTER 40

Then Consolidate:
The Nuances That Stop the Stalls

Decisions are not always made logically. Often, they
are made with emotion and then supported with logic.

—A Nancy Timely Tip

Tribal Types and Decisions

Tribal Types®

Getting that decision can be rewarding—and frustrating! Many factors can affect decision-making, including those listed on the next page.

- Emotions
- Their trust level with you
- The belief that what you offer will help with their POWNs
- Budget
- Internal politics

Don't ignore emotions' impact on decision-making. Tap into what you learned about their emotional hot buttons, sense of urgency, and Risks and Rewards in the *Investigate* step to address and influence the emotional and logical components.

I've observed that decisions are not always made logically. Often, they are made with emotion and then supported with logic. The emotions can be positive or negative; some people move forward with excitement or joy, while others may be driven more by fear or other negative emotions.

You impact the prospect's decision-making as well. Some prospects won't make a decision without your proactive approach and confidence in asking for a commitment. Others don't want you to complicate the process and want you to get out of their way. Tribal Types customs provide insight into how different people approach and reach decisions. This insight allows you to vary your approach in asking for the decision.

Achievers

Achievers make quick and impulsive decisions. They fear being taken advantage of or failing to achieve something on time because of a delay. When they hear something that resonates with them, they are ready to "just do it," as the Nike brand slogan says. While this helps you secure a quick decision, you can encounter some pitfalls. For example, they may have wrong expectations, or others in their family may challenge the decision.

To aid Achievers at decision time:

🍤 Provide only the most important information to them

🍤 Don't overcomplicate the decision-making process

🍤 Make it easy for them by taking care of the details or paperwork, if possible

🍤 Let them know that slowing down now to address other information may prove beneficial later

🍤 Ask, "What would you like to do next?"

Commanders

Commanders like to make the right decision, and they fear being wrong. Their need to be right might mean that decision-making is a long process that includes lots of facts, evidence, analysis, and more analysis. However, this need can also be a blind spot that blocks out relevant information—even if the information supports what they want to do. Commanders like options and the ability to compare services. They also like the final decision to be their idea so the opinions of others carry little weight. They need to make a sound and correct decision, but their decisions aren't always as logical as they believe.

To aid Commanders at decision time:

🍤 Provide the information they need, preferably in print

🍤 Take a logical and organized approach to the process that leads to the decision

🍤 Use quantifiable information whenever possible to describe the value provided by your solution and the return on their investment

🍤 Present options for them to select from

🍤 Ask, "What other information would be helpful as you weigh your options?"

Reflectors

Reflectors need time to make a decision. Because they don't like risk and want to be careful, they need information, detail, and others' input to comfortably make the decision. The bigger the decision, the more information, detail, and input they will need. The "buy now or you lose out" approach does not work well with them, and they will decide *not* to do something if pushed. The delay in making a final decision can be costly for them, as they won't get the help and benefits you provide for a long time. Reflectors fear change and instability, which can make every decision feel like a risky one. They worry that something will go wrong after they decide and then they will be stuck.

To aid Reflectors at decision time:

🖋 Clarify the process of what happens after a decision is made

🖋 If they work with others on your team, introduce them directly or through a bio

🖋 Set expectations and be clear on what decision you are seeking

🖋 Be patient but assertive. Though they need time to make the decision, they also appreciate a timeline that forces them to make the decision

🖋 Ask, "How can I support you as you finalize your decision?"

🖋 Touch base with them more often than with the other Tribes

Expressers

Expressers make a lot of "on-the-spot" decisions, and they may reverse many of them as well. They may make a decision when talking with an advisor if it satisfies them and the people with them at that time. If contrary opinions or ideas surface soon after, they can be easily swayed to change their decision. The opinions of the other people involved matter to them. You, the people on your team, and the people affected by the decision are important drivers in a decision.

Be careful; Expressers may tell you how much they like you and your service, tell you how great you are, and how much they like this or that. *This isn't necessarily a buying signal.* They don't want to hurt your feelings. Also, Expressers' decisions are often highly emotional, and they can be "oversold." Further, Expressers fear making an unpopular decision that will affect how others feel about them.

To aid Expressers at decision time:

🖐 Stay in touch with them to keep you and your solution in their mind, and plan for time to be social in your conversations rather than "all business"

🖐 Offer your opinion. They may even ask "What would you do?" or "Do you use this?"

🖐 Find out who else needs to be involved, and involve them as early on as possible in the sales process

🖐 Appeal to their visual learning tendency by using tangible resources to show a story they can put themselves into

🖐 Highlight and condense the most important items for them, avoiding lengthy reports or detailed handouts. Then equip them with more details to "sell it" to others—spouse, partner, family member, lawyer, and so on—internally if they need to

🖐 Ask, "Who else will be impacted by this?" Positive opinions from others will spur them on; negative ones are better out in the open so you can address them (collaboratively, of course)

Recognizing the customs of each Tribal Type helps you to address their logical and emotional needs when making decisions. Adjust how you work with the prospect through all the WIIFT® steps and then ask for the decision.

Confidently securing the decision or commitment moves stalled opportunities forward, increases your closing success, and strengthens the value you bring to the sales process.

A decision has been made! Either you have a new client

—congratulations to you and the client!—or the prospect committed to moving to the next step. Great progress! Now, it's time for the hard work of setting up the successful relationship or next step.

Action 4: Identify the Next Steps with Specifics

Whether the prospect makes a final decision to work together or commits to take the next step, their choice sets off a list of to-dos.

If they make a final decision to work together, that decision is just the beginning of your real work. Their satisfaction or dissatisfaction with your service starts now!

If they decide to take the next step, setting the expectations and actions for each of you is just as important.

Missed expectations cause nearly every client complaint and client resignation. To set the initial post-decision expectations, you need to clearly identify *who* is doing *what* by *when* and *how*.

Identify the next steps that you and the prospect will take after the conversation. These steps could be creating an agreement and payment setup, scheduling the next conversation, sharing information, or many other tasks.

Clarify implementation specifics and future communication preferences and timelines to keep you moving forward. Setting the right expectations after a decision has been made eliminates redundancy and lack of action, thereby speeding up the value-giving process.

Some of the next steps you may need to clarify:

🖋 If your prospect commits to a follow-up meeting with you and their spouse or partner, identify the date of the meeting, its objectives, and any information that needs to be exchanged before then.

🖋 If the prospect has agreed to work with you, clearly outline the exact next steps both of you need to take. To make it a solid plan, include who, what, when, and how.

Once the next steps are identified, secure a commitment from them on their actions. And to check relevancy of the next actions, ask them a question such as, "Which one of you will be the lead in this?" "What might get in the way of getting us the documents?" or "How can we support you in taking those actions?"

Action 5: Close the Conversation

Then Consolidate ends with a close ... every time! The close is your final statements or words before ending the conversation—and this closure counts.

To close the conversation and minimize potential buyer's remorse, let them know they have made a sound or good decision and again restate the value—how their POWNs will be resolved.

Personalize your final statements with specific and relevant comments such as:

- "Thanks for allowing us to _____."
- "I appreciate the time you have given us to _____."
- "I appreciate your arranging a meeting next week with _____."
- "Please do not hesitate to contact me if you have any questions."

You will keep future opportunities open with an invitation and/or question such as:

- "How else might we help you?"
- "What else would you like to discuss?"
- "Please know that you can contact me via email or phone whenever you need."
- "When should I follow up to see if all is going as planned?"
- "What's the best way to stay in contact with you?"

End your conversation as positively as it started with phrases like "Congratulations," "Thank you," or "I appreciate _____." Include a specific and personal reason why you are congratulating or thanking them. According to a 2010 study from the *Journal of Marketing*, flattery works!

TIMELY TIP

The power of a sincere "congratulations!" is underestimated. Congratulating your prospect on a decision or commitment is a powerful way to strengthen their confidence that they've made the best decision in moving forward. To make it more powerful, send a note of congratulations after the conversation.

Then Consolidate is the final step to successfully bring your sales conversation to closure. Yet keep in mind that one run-through of WIIFT is often not enough if you have a multistep sales process.

WIIFT is a conversation framework and a strategic road map to track your major stopping points within multiple sales cycles. Follow the 5 steps of WIIFT in every prospect conversation to advance or make your sale.

CHAPTER 41

Quick Tips and Best Practices for Consolidating Your Conversations

As you implement the *Then Consolidate* step, use these quick tips and best practices, from advisors who have completed the Genuine Sales 12-week course. There's also a success story to show the concepts in action.

Quick Tips

- Pay attention to the emotional and logical factors that impact decision-making. Different fears come into play, and your ability to Stop, Drop, and Roll with any final concerns will alleviate those fears.

- Summarize and then assertively ask for the decision. Then pause for them to respond. Forward movement and action is the goal—for you and your prospective client.

- Clearly identify specific next steps, and don't leave anything hanging or assumed.

- Follow up with a written confirmation of the next actions after the conversation. This is especially appreciated by Commanders and Reflectors and may be necessary to keep the Expressers and Achievers on track.

- Eliminate Decision Questions that ask for two competing decisions. Being vague or unclear about what you are asking for may give them an easy out.

- Clarify best communication preferences at the end of conversations, for you and Them.

- Close your conversation with a personalized statement or invitation to keep the door open to future opportunities.

Advisor's Best Practices and Tips for Consolidating the Conversation

- Write out Readiness Questions in advance.

- Practice the 3-Step Finish before appointments.

- Practice the *Then Consolidate* conversation.

- Check for readiness and restate the value.

- Confirm the value of your solution without being repetitive and saying the same thing you said two minutes ago in *Facilitate.*

- Be sure to confirm the value—don't skip that step.

- Craft several powerful "Asks."

- Check decision readiness.

- Identify next steps.

- Ask for the decision.

- Be direct with Decision Questions.

- Always get a commitment.

🗲 Always get next steps. Don't let them just drift off.

🗲 Show that you're interested and that you're going to follow up about a specific action on a specific date.

Success!

I had a call with a client at the end of last week, and I asked more Readiness and Decision Questions. I probed the prospect to see where they were in deciding.

The prospect was on the fence. I asked what else I could provide to help her make a decision. She mentioned more information and material would be helpful. The outcome is that we scheduled a follow-up call because she got what she needed. The follow-up call is next week with the objective to get a more definitive answer about working together.

–DANIELLE ARLOTTA, BROOKLYN PLANS

PART III

Tips and Tools to Be a Collaborative Sales Converter

CHAPTER 42

The Factors That Make or Break Your Sales

"The biggest game you will ever play is the game in your mind. Master your mind, master your world."

—Kevin Abdulrahman, business speaker, coach, and consultant

Will You or Won't You Succeed? It's Your Choice

What does it really take to be successful in sales, especially financial sales? Is selling an art or a science? Are salespeople born or made? Is knowledge or skill more important in selling success? What is the *one* characteristic all advisors must have? What do I have to do to be good at sales? These are just some of the great debates in the sales community.

These debates generate so many opinions that it's impossible to select one definitive answer to any of them. What is consistent, though, is that the responses to these queries include specific competence and confidence factors. I call these the *Skill* and *Will* factors for sales success.

Skill and Will®: The Dynamic Duo of Sales Success

Skill and *Will*, an easily remembered phrase referring to the factors of top performance in any field, is the dynamic duo of sales success.

Skill is your competence: the knowledge of *what* to do and *how* to effectively put that knowledge into productive and consistent action.

Skills can be learned, observed, and easily evaluated from the outside. Most of this book has focused on this—skills in collaborative WIIFT conversations adjusted for the Tribal Types.

Skill is important, yet equally important is the *Will* to perform.

Will is the confidence and drive to take action; it is *why* you do what you do. It's internally based and invisible to the outside world.

In most teams, I find that the advisor who knows the most is often *not* the advisor who sells the most. The most successful advisors are those who have the required knowledge *and* take the necessary actions to source and convert clients through their *Will*.

Some of their behaviors include the following:

✺ Work on lead generation efforts consistently.

✺ Prepare for conversations and overall strategy.

✺ Use a consistent and collaborative conversation approach.

✺ Build relationships outside their company.

✺ Contact appropriate prospects daily.

✺ Ask for decisions.

✺ Follow up.

✺ Continue to learn.

Committing to these actions and consistently taking them is impacted more by the *Will* factor than the *Skill* factor. The *Will* factor amplifies sales *Skills*. Take two advisors with the same *Skill* and I can accurately predict that the one with a stronger *Will* factor will perform better.

The *Will* factor's impact can be observed in the Dianna Nyad story. As someone who loves to swim and be in or near water, I couldn't wait to track Dianna's progress in her Cuba-to-Florida swim in 2013.

Dianna is an American author, journalist, motivational speaker, and long-distance swimmer. Her swimming accomplishments are many, and her first world record was earned by swimming around the island of Manhattan in less than 8 hours.

Yet that record is not the best indicator of her *Will* to achieve a goal. Dianna had already proven she had the skills to swim long distances in open water. Yet her attempts to complete the 110-mile Cuba-to-Florida swim tested her Will. She made her first attempt at 28 years old in 1978 and was pulled from her swim due to high winds.

For decades she moved on with life. Then at 60 years old, she tackled the 110-mile challenge again. She rebuilt her skill and attempted four more times before finally completing the journey in 2013.

Her Will allowed her to remain focused, stay the course of the grueling planning and training, and have the right team to ensure her safety. How many times do you think she was ready to give up during all those years?

The Success Drivers of Top Advisors

Being "in the zone" is typically a sports reference, yet it can also refer to maximizing productivity and success in work and in life. The "zone" is a state of total focus and effortless performance where your knowledge and skill merge.

Advisors in the zone of success are driven to succeed. This success then builds more success, and it may seem as if they have luck or a magic touch. But as author Coleman Cox said, "I'm a great believer in luck. The harder I work, the more of it I seem to have."

Action is necessary for being in the zone. While most advisors will intellectually agree with the tools, steps, and behaviors outlined in this book, what happens next with that knowledge—action or inaction—is the difference between mediocre and stellar performance.

The *Will* factor is complex, consisting of several components that I call Success Drivers™. Strengthening these components (the Drivers) propels you to actions, results, and success.

In studying the top performers among the thousands of advisors I have worked with, I have noticed four common Drivers that help explain why some advisors do what is necessary to succeed and others don't. (I say "help explain" because the dynamics of sales success and the uniqueness of each advisor make this topic neither as simple nor formulaic as presented here.)

The Success Drivers model shown in Graphic 42–1 illustrates the Drivers—Integrated Beliefs (Self, Value, Role), Goal Transparency, Initiative, and Emotional Intelligence—and their relationship to each other.

Graphic 42-1

Meet the Drivers of Success

Success starts at the center of the model with Beliefs, a multifaceted internal Driver that integrates the beliefs you have in *yourself*, in your *role*, and in the value of your solution. This Driver connects with the other three Success Drivers: Goal Transparency, Initiative, and Emotional Intelligence.

The four Drivers give some substance to the *Will* factor. Let's look at them in more detail.

Integrated Beliefs

Confidence is often cited as a key characteristic of top-performing advisors. Does this confidence come from their success, or has their success created their confidence? Probably both. Confidence comes from the internal beliefs about *who they are*, *what they do*, and *why their solution is valuable to others*. The integration of these three beliefs directly impacts their actions.

Integrated Beliefs are three beliefs that combine to drive Goal Transparency, Initiative, and Emotional Intelligence. Their integration positively or negatively impacts their effect on your actions.

Belief in self means you have confidence in your abilities and skills to succeed. The value you personally bring to your prospects and customers is reflected in this belief. You are integral to the total value your prospects receive when they decide to work with you.

To gauge your level of belief in yourself, answer these questions:

- Do you want to be successful?
- Do you see yourself being successful in sales?
- Do you believe that you have, or that you can develop, the skills and attitudes to be successful?
- Do you believe that you give value to your customers and prospects in the sales process and beyond?

Self-confidence affects your prospect's confidence as well. Prospects may identify lack of confidence as weakness or inability. They may also think you are a waste of their time. If they sense your lack of confidence, they won't feel confident in you or your recommendation.

Belief in role is the belief in the value of your sales role to your company, your prospects, and yourself. A strong belief in your role leads to feeling good about what you do. As mentioned in the introduction to this book, reluctant advisors may have a low belief in the value of selling, which negatively impacts the actions and activities needed to succeed.

To gauge the level of belief in your role, listen to how you describe what you do. Do you describe it as a "just" position? Do you say, "I'm just in sales," "I'm just the person peddling this stuff," or "I'm just the liaison"? If you don't see that you are integral to the Win[3] through your efforts and role, neither will the prospect—nor will your boss.

Belief in value is the belief in your service's value in relation to the cost to secure the service. Your belief that the service is worth more than its cost matters. For instance, during my time as a distributor for a training product, many of us believed a new product had been prematurely launched and that the quality of the solution was not up to the standards that our customers expected and valued. No matter how much the marketing department and the president tried to convince us of the product's value and threw incentives at us to sell this new course, many of us continued to sell the old one. Because we did not believe in the value of the new version, we could not sell or relate its value to prospects and clients. Sales suffered.

Have you noticed that it is easier for you to sell some of your products or services than others? If you look closely, you might find that you have high personal belief in the value of the solutions you are most successful with. That's the effect of the belief in value.

Integrated Beliefs are the core of the Success Drivers model and describe the importance of beliefs in who, what, and why. They are reflected in the passion you have for yourself, your profession, and your service. Advisors with strong Integrated Beliefs have confidence and are driven to help as many prospects as possible gain access to their service.

Because the beliefs integrate, when you strengthen any one of the beliefs, you positively affect the others. The opposite is also true; if any one of the beliefs is low, the other beliefs suffer as well.

Goal Transparency

Goal Transparency is more than being goal-oriented or goal-driven. It means having written goals that are specific, measurable, and visible to you and others.

Transparency is demonstrated when your goals are visible to you and others in print, in your actions, and in your words. By sharing your goals and your plans to reach them with your stakeholders, you make the invisible visible and you add accountability. A regular review of your goals also keeps them relevant, timely, and valid.

Top performers' goals are transparent. The transparency of their goals gives them stronger accountability to focus on the actions necessary to reach them. They are up front about what they want to accomplish. If you can help them, great. If you can't, move out of their way! They know where they are headed and will move obstacles that keep them from reaching their goals.

Goal Transparency is key to strengthening your results, your commitment, and the other three Drivers.

Initiative

Initiative is the self-directed, personal, proactive energy you spend every day. Those with Initiative focus their energy toward proactive and productive activities that help them complete what is important.

Essentially, Initiative is motivation. Because it is internal, only *you* can motivate yourself. Contrary to what many believe, others can't motivate you. Only *you* can find the motivators that rev up your energy.

Author Daniel Pink addresses this complexity in his 2009 book *Drive*. He explains that some are motivated internally to achieve high levels of performance; others are motivated by external rewards. To increase your Initiative, find your personal motivators and then focus on proactive and productive activities to get you where you need or want to go more efficiently.

Top performers take Initiative each day. They face the same priority challenges as everyone else and don't necessarily enjoy some of the mundane parts of selling—like writing follow-up notes, preparation, and plugging information into the company database—any more than others do. What they do, though, is Initiate action on these non-desirables or figure out a way to get them done through other resources, because they know these activities will help them succeed. They focus on the most productive activities and get more done to maximize their time and energy.

Emotional Intelligence

Now for the real stuff—the impact of your emotions on your actions! And boy, do emotions come into play on a daily basis in financial services!

Emotional Intelligence is the awareness of and ability to manage your emotions and their impact on your actions. The importance of this Driver is supported by a research study which found that top sales performers scored markedly higher on emotional intelligence than low performers and that this high correlation held regardless of age, education level, experience, or other demographic factors.[10]

---

[10] George C. Chipain, "Emotional intelligence and its relationship with sales success" (2003). College of Education Theses and Dissertations. 126. https://via.library.depaul.edu/soe_etd/126

After all, selling is a tough part of advisory work. Rejection and success can happen within minutes of each other, and the roller-coaster of emotions that comes with sales efforts is not always easy to ride.

While "most salespeople know what to do," says Colleen Stanley, author of *Emotional Intelligence for Sales Success*, "during stressful selling situations, emotions take over rather than good selling and communication skills. It's the classic knowing and doing gap."

Thus, strong Emotional Intelligence leads to consistent action, and emotionally intelligent advisors don't let their emotions negatively impact their actions, activity level, or confidence in asking for meetings and decisions.

Colleen shares that emotionally intelligent people are self-aware. "They know what emotion they are feeling, why they are feeling the emotion, and how that emotion affects how they show up."

Pausing to acknowledge success, either big or little, is also important to a strong Emotional Intelligence. And advisors don't do this enough, especially those who are solo! You spend time noting what you didn't do without pausing to process the positives. Receiving little hits of dopamine by pausing and processing your successes will build confidence and commitment to the sales activities.

Emotional Intelligence is connected to Goal Transparency and Initiative. As Daniel Pink writes in *Drive*, "On days when workers have the sense they're making headway in their jobs, or when they receive support that helps them overcome obstacles, their emotions are most positive and their drive to succeed is at its peak."

Emotionally intelligent advisors are aware of their response to outside influences and don't let obstacles, bad days, negative experiences, and rejections stop them. They keep on productively and proactively making decisions and doing what is necessary, even when they don't want to. Their awareness of and ability to productively manage their emotions is key to their success.

* * * * *

How do these Success Drivers play out in the real world of sales? Advisors who understand their personal *Skill* and *Will* and access their unique strengths and preferences generally grow their client base faster than others.

Some advisors are more focused on their *Skill* while others have enough *Will* to drive them to act and make sales. Advisors with a record of long-term growth use a balance of *Skill* and *Will* to consistently achieve their goals.

You say you're not a "born" salesperson? That might be good because whether you started with a positive mindset about selling doesn't count as much as whether you are willing to develop yourself into a business professional who can sell.

Strength in the four Success Drivers—Integrated Beliefs, Goal Transparency, Initiative, and Emotional Intelligence—drive the right actions that propel you to results and success. If your drive for success is not as high as you would like, you can build each of these Success Drivers with the Quick Tips in the next chapter.

CHAPTER 43

Quick Tips to Build Your Drive to Succeed

Please review and revisit these Quick Tips, Best Practices, and a Success story for strengthening your Success Drivers.

Quick Tips

- Build belief in yourself: take time to document your successes for your reference and for performance review time.

- Build belief in your role: Regularly consume helpful sales information that resonates with you (forums, industry publications, blogs, podcasts, social media posts, conference sessions, etc.). Participate in ongoing sales development.

- Build belief in the value of your solution: Make a list of the value your prospects and clients receive from you and your solution. Make note of what your clients thank you for.

- Strengthen Goal Transparency: Identify goals and the plan of action necessary to achieve them, share your goals with stakeholders, and take action to achieve your goals.

🖋 Increase your Initiative: Stop procrastinating and act! In his book *Eat that Frog!*, author Brian Tracy suggests that you complete the toughest task first each day to release the energy you would spend on avoiding or thinking about the task the rest of the day.

🖋 Boost your Emotional Intelligence: Start a Smile File—a bright yellow file folder to store any notes of thanks, appreciation, job well done, recognition, or successes. On days when your emotional intelligence is low, review the contents to remind yourself of the value you bring.

🖋 Use the Success Drivers for diagnosing roadblocks that lead to lack of confidence, procrastination in sales efforts, and regular fee discounting.

Advisor's Best Practices and Tips to Increase Drive

Integrated Beliefs

🖋 Journal to strengthen Integrated Beliefs and examine what's going on

🖋 Keep a success journal, focus on the things that go well, don't dwell on the negative, keep a positive mindset

🖋 Write and say positive affirmations

🖋 Talk with others who are successful and/or more experienced

🖋 Focus on manageable and healthy daily goals

🖋 Find a partner to discuss and celebrate little wins

🖋 Keep a list of statements from clients that tell you how much of a difference you've made

🖋 Don't downplay your role in success, and don't focus only on negative outcomes and self-blame

Goal Transparency

🖊 Write goals and revisit on a regular basis

🖊 Keep goals visible so you see them daily

🖊 Break goals into smaller pieces and review every week

🖊 Prioritize your actions/goals to be clear on what is moving the needle

🖊 Celebrate when goals are reached

Initiative

🖊 Set up a checklist before the week begins

🖊 Find a strong *Why* and revisit it often

🖊 Like the Nike motto—*Just do it*

🖊 Exercise

🖊 Make sure you are resting when you're tired

🖊 Check who you are spending your time with

🖊 Listen to music to add energy if needed

Emotional Intelligence

🖊 Take time to have a "pity party" and feel/acknowledge setbacks

🖊 Meditate

🖊 Exercise

🖊 Use deep breathing techniques

🖊 Associate with positive people

🖊 Remind yourself of the big picture

🖊 Write morning pages to figure out what is going on in your brain

Success!

I have increased my confidence and belief in myself and in my role. Before adopting the Genuine Sales® (collaborative) approach, I knew the value that we provided but felt really uncomfortable explaining it. Going through this course has made me feel more comfortable talking through it with prospects.

–JEN PRITCHARD, CFP, COLUMBIA, MISSOURRI

I have learned to do a daily check-in on my sense of personal Belief in Self and Belief in Role from the Success Drivers. This increased self-awareness has given me a lot more confidence as I talk to prospective clients.

–ED COAMBS, HEALTHY LOVE AND MONEY

CHAPTER 44

What's in Your Toolbox?

"If you give people tools, (and they use)
their natural ability and their curiosity, they will
develop things in ways that will surprise you very
much beyond what you might have expected."

—Bill Gates

Though you don't carry a hammer, saw, or screwdriver to work, the right tools get the job done better. That's why I'm summarizing the top no-tech tools that will help you make Win^3 sales more efficiently and effectively.

A tool is anything that helps you get something done. In today's world, the term "tools" is synonymous with software and gadgets. However, far too many people spend many thousands of dollars on new tools and technology and some advisors spend so much time with the latest gadget that it detracts from their selling activities. While gadgetry and technology are helpful—and at times even lifesavers— some advisors continue to do very well with just a paper, pen, and Excel spreadsheet.

Though some of you who are committed to the latest apps on tablets or smartphones may find my opinion too simplistic, the specific tools you use don't matter nearly as much as *how* you use them.

Whether you are a gadget person or prefer paper and pen, the tools you pull out of your toolbox—your briefcase, hard drive, or mind—need to work for you.

In this chapter, I will feature 3 sales conversation preparation tools that will help you get your "job" in sales done more productively and efficiently.

I have seen far too many people spend many thousands of dollars on new "tools and technology." I've also seen advisors who spend so much time with the latest gadget that it detracts from their selling activities.

What works is identifying and then committing to the consistent use of the tools in your toolbox.

Sales Conversation Preparation Tools

You've already been given 2 sales conversation preparation tools in this book: the Quick Prep Tool and the Tribal Types Tool. Now, this chapter will introduce some additional ideas for effectively incorporating these tools into your preparation.

Quick Prep Tool

As English logician and novelist Lewis Carroll wrote in *Alice in Wonderland*,

"Would you tell me, please, which way I ought to walk from here?"
"That depends a good deal on where you want to get to," said the Cat.
"I don't much care where——" said Alice.
"Then it doesn't matter which way you walk," said the Cat.

Fortunately, you do have a "way to walk" when you use the Quick Prep Tool shown in Graphic 44-1: you are going into a productive conversation with your prospects.

WIIFT Quick Prep Tool™
for Financial Advisors

Date: _____

Name (All names and roles, if applicable)   Tribal Type©(s)

WAIT Objective(s) for conversation

Prospect's Need to know (plus POWNs if known)   Need to knows (What I need to learn)

Value and benefits important to Them (How will I differentiate our solution?)

INITIATE 3-Step Start notes (Greet, Explain why, Ask time/connection questions to open)

NOTES

INVESTIGATE 4-Point Questions to uncover POWNs (Problems, Opportunities, Wants, and Needs)

Today   NOTES

Tomorrow

Risk

Reward

FACILITATE Possible recommendation(s) or information to be shared with Whats to WiifTs

NOTES

Possible objections or concerns with notes for
Acknowledge, Ask questions, Answers with WiifT

Objections   Ask Questions

THEN CONSOLIDATE Decision or commitment desired and 3-Step Finish Notes
(Check for Readiness, Confirm, Ask). Next steps and expectations to set

NOTES

Follow-up Action Items

What   Who   When   How

Financial Advisor version ©Sales Pro Insider, Inc. 2009, 2013, 2015, 2023 Nancy Bleeke 414.235.3064
This is an individually licensed product. No copies or use permitted if not a licensed user of Genuine Sales.

SalesProInsider™

Graphic 44-1
WIIFT Quick Prep

Quick Research™

Date: _____

Access research sources to help understand this prospect(s). Review any information collected from emails, CRM, online questionnaires, social networking groups, LinkedIn, company or industry forums, "Google" etc.

Research notes – Who are they? Where do they work? What's their presence online? Who are they connected with? Who is in their family? What do they do for fun? What types of groups or affiliations do they have?

For this prospect(s), what is in alignment with our services? What potential value do we offer?

What specific information do I need to qualify this prospect? Quantitative information: assets, income, career, family stage, etc. Qualitative information: willingness to change, take advice, collaborate, work with an advisor, pay for services, follow-through, personality fit, etc.

For a business prospect, use the following section to guide your research -

Review company's website, LinkedIn profiles of key people, brochures, annual reports, and marketing documents for useful information about:

Mission or value statement

Key stakeholders (names, roles, backgrounds)

Recent company business news (financial results, news releases)

Specific business goals (new markets, expansion, returns to stakeholders, personal goals, etc.)

Financial Advisor version ©Sales Pro Insider, Inc. 2009, 2013, 2015, 2023 Nancy Bleeke 414.235.3064
This is an individually licensed product. No copies or use permitted if not a licensed user of Genuine Sales.

Graphic 44-2
Quick Research

Whether you believe preparation is a good idea or that it is just for rookies, I can't stress enough that the discipline of preparing for leading collaborative conversations makes *everyone* more productive and efficient.

The Quick Prep Tool has 2 pages with specific purposes and values for you:

✒ WIIFT Quick Prep provides a guide to prepare for the entire WIIFT conversation.

✒ Quick Research outlines research prompts for new prospects.

You can download a copy of the Quick Prep Tool from *www. conversationsthatsell.com*. Or, if you want to write really small, copy the pages from this book.

Complete the WIIFT Quick Prep page for every conversation you initiate—whether prospect or COI. The steps of WIIFT are outlined to guide you through preparing for each step. As of writing this book in 2024, AI tools are newer and yet pervasive. We haven't yet incorporated the Quick Prep Tool into an AI program, but I am sure you can.

To use this tool effectively, begin with the end in mind by first *identifying the objective* of the conversation. Then write notes in the remaining sections for each step of the WIIFT conversation. During your conversation, there's space for you to make notes from the *Investigate* and follow-up items.

After your conversation, complete the paperwork trail by noting your follow-up action items on the last line. If you have a customer database, input the relevant information directly into your system while it's fresh.

The Quick Research page guides you through productive research items. For opportunities that need more planning, complete this side *before* the WIIFT Quick Prep page. The information you gather from this page's various research prompts ensures a relevant conversation for the prospect, saves both of you time, and sets you apart from all the other advisors calling on that prospect.

Tribal Types Tool

The Tribal Types model helps you to communicate and work with your prospects in the way *they* prefer, their customs. Identifying their preferred communication and working customs allows you to adapt your conversations to make every question you ask and every bit of information you share timely and relevant.

The customs for each of the four Tribal Types are easy to learn. Yet our personal biases and quick judgments may complicate our ability to identify the Tribe. The Tribal Types Tool in Graphic 44–3 provides a quick way to identify the Tribal Type of your prospect (or colleague or sales manager).

Tribal Types Tool™

Name: _____

Write the name of the person who you are assessing at the top.

Read through the list of 18 descriptors under each Type.

Circle or click on the words or phrases that best describe the person you are assessing.

Write the number of circles for each Type in the space labeled "Total."

Achiever

TOTAL /18

FOCUS	OBSERVED	WORDS USED
Achievement	Results oriented	Time
Results	Need to achieve	Bottom-line
Ideas	Many priorities	When?
Action	Completion	Net
Awards	Recognition	Make it quick
Quick	May miss details	Now

Attention

Results

TOTAL /18

Expresser

FOCUS	OBSERVED	WORDS USED
Stories	Verbal	I feel
Approval	Ask oriented	Like
People	Social	Happy
Emotions	More talking than action	Great
Sharing	Need to be with others	Awesome
Outward	Appearances matter	What do others say?

Commander

FOCUS	OBSERVED	WORDS USED
Data	Order	Review
Methods	Analytical	Think
Accuracy	Need for hard facts	Compare
Control	Tell oriented	How do you know?
Inward	Guarded emotions	Research shows
Facts	Assesses/Analyzes	Why?

TOTAL /18

Reflector

People

Process

FOCUS	OBSERVED	WORDS USED
Details	Precise	How?
People	Involve others	Process
Information	Need for details	I feel
Safety	Consistency	Don't want to rush
Security	Prefers tried & true	Are you sure?
Internal	Careful word choice	Who else?

TOTAL /18

Nancy Bieeke Noël 414.235.3064

SalesProInsider Inc.

Graphic 44-3
Tribal Types Tool

To use the Tribal Types Tool, follow these directions:

🌀 Write the name of the person you are assessing in the line on the top right

🌀 Read through the list of 18 descriptors under each Tribe

🌀 Circle the words or phrases that best describe the person you are assessing

🌀 Write the total number of circles for each Tribe in the space labeled "Total"

The Tribal Type with the highest score is considered the dominant Tribe. If two Tribal Types have equal scores, then both sets of customs are important to that person.

People are a mix; it is highly unusual for a person to fit all 18 descriptors for their Tribal Type. Yet it is very likely for customs from all four of the Tribal Types to apply to that person.

I've discussed many strategies for selling and working with each of the Tribal Types in detail in Chapters 9 through 14. While preparing for your conversations, incorporate the specific customs into the types of connection and discussion questions you will ask, the level of detail you will discuss and divulge, the types of materials you have available, the time you will allot for the conversation, and the level of personal relationship you want or need to build.

If you don't have any clues to work from prior to your first conversation, ask people who have worked with or connected with the prospect for ideas on how to best work with them. Then complete the Tribal Types Tool immediately *following* your conversation to prepare for your follow-up and future conversations.

Download a printable PDF of the Tribal Types Tool from the QR Code:

The Most Important Sales Tool: You!

Paper or power tools don't convert prospects. *You* do. You are the most important tool in your toolbox. Use your time, efforts, skills, and strengths effectively to gain higher efficiency, lower stress, higher productivity, greater happiness, and stronger job security.

To best utilize your strengths, you need to know what they are. Regular assessment of your abilities and what works and doesn't work for you is smart practice. Assessing your strengths for the *Skill* and *Will* factors discussed in Chapters 42 and 43 also provides a platform for you to build from.

In addition to this, you can use another tool to assess your strengths and opportunities:

⟆ *The Sales Survey.* The Sales Survey at *www.conversationsthatsell.com* allows you to self-assess and identify your benchmark of the *Skill* and *Will* components. The survey results make it easy for you to capitalize on your strengths—and suggest which of the components you may want to develop further.

Download a printable PDF of the Sales Survey from the QR Code:

Use the information from your assessment to pinpoint your self-development opportunities. For maximum impact, choose 2 or 3 specific *Skill* or *Will* components from the assessment to focus your development efforts. However, don't get caught in the trap of thinking that you need to tackle the lowest-scoring items. Often, you will benefit more when you focus on developing your best and second-best strengths than the lowest-scoring items.

Quick Tips to Use What's in Your Toolbox

🎣 Prepare for every conversation on paper or screen. Use the WIIFT® Quick Prep Tool to plan your conversation flow.

🎣 Make time for researching new prospects, large opportunities, or stalled opportunities. The Quick Research guide provides thought-starters for where to begin your research.

🎣 Use the Tribal Types Tool to adjust how you work and sell with your prospects.

🎣 Stay current with the technology tools available to you for managing your sales activities and prospects. Then use what you have.

While AI is all the rage in 2024, who knows what it will be in 2030?

🔥 Identify your benchmark for the *Skill* and *Will* factors. Keep doing what works well. For the components you want to build or change, develop a personal growth plan.

The value of the tools in your toolbox increases when you consistently incorporate them into managing your activities and preparing for your conversations. You will get more from your time and efforts, and working smarter leaves you with more time and energy.

CHAPTER 45

Now What? Action Time!

"A good plan violently executed Now is better than a perfect plan next week."

—General George S. Patton

Throughout this book, I've mentioned how busy everyone is—your prospects, clients, COIs, and *you*! And that busyness leads to full days—mostly spent reacting to the demands of everyone else. To make sure you aren't lost in all the reactive activity, you need to be more purposeful with your time and actions.

Ernest Hemingway wrote, "Never mistake motion for action." Even though you may put forth great effort and fill your days with activity, a scattershot approach is ineffective and benefits neither you nor your prospects.

Purposeful, focused action stems from knowing what to do with your *Skill*, and then tapping into your *Will* to do it. I'll end this book with a few tips to help you "get to it."

Getting Started

Create a schedule for tackling the chapters—one per week—and schedule time each week to read and follow the tips for each chapter.

Identify and commit to a SMART (Specific, Measurable, Achievable, Relevant, and Time-Bound) sales goal. Will this guarantee you will reach your goal on time, within budget, and with your sanity intact? No. The guarantee comes with accountability, transparency, commitment, and support.

Involving Stakeholders

Share your goals with a stakeholder—someone who cares about or is affected by the outcome of your goal, such as a spouse, colleague, supervisor, or friend—to make your goal transparent and provide accountability for you to reach it. It's much easier to delay working on a goal that no one else knows about. Knowing that your stakeholders will ask you about progress often adds the nudge to get moving on it. Stakeholders also support you in the following ways:

- Clarifying the outcome with you to make sure it is specific enough for you to know whether you reach it.

- Identifying other actions that can get you there quicker or easier and eliminate some of the roadblocks.

- Supporting you along the way.

- Contributing to resources or helping with actions.

- Celebrating your progress and ultimate success!

Involving a stakeholder is a powerful way to increase the likelihood of achieving your goal. So why don't more people identify stakeholders and ask for their support? They tell me they don't want to burden someone else. Though understandable, they're overlooking the benefits a stakeholder receives from supporting or assisting them with their goals.

Stakeholders benefit from the sense of satisfaction of helping someone else succeed, a boost that helps them achieve a goal of their own (there is power in being with others who are succeeding and achieving), and an opportunity to learn from or be exposed to something new.

Celebrating Progress

And finally, it's important to take the time to pause and celebrate. Take time to reward yourself. As an Achiever, I don't pause enough when I complete a goal. I move right into the next one. Thank goodness my stakeholders stop me and hold me accountable to celebrate.

If you want to increase your motivation to complete the necessary actions, find ways to celebrate progress, not just the final outcome. Don't hold out on acknowledging your progress or success because you are so focused on what isn't yet done. That trap will drain your energy. Find ways to enjoy your journey and acknowledge or celebrate the milestones along the way.

THE WRAP-UP

There you have it—many prompts to get you going in building the business you want, working with the people you want, and living the life you want.

Now what? Most importantly, the key is to get started.

I've given you a lot of information about how to skillfully and willfully have conversations that count. And although information is powerful, it is only powerful when put to good use. To ensure you benefit from the time you invested in reading the book, I end with a quote by Walt Disney: "The way to get started is to quit talking and begin doing."

Quick Tips to Get the Most From this Book

⚡ Set a realistic goal. Then make a plan for achieving the goal.

⚡ Commit to the goal, verbally and in writing. Recommit monthly.

⚡ Identify the *Why*—your real reward for achieving the goal.

⚡ Share with a stakeholder.

⚡ Take action! Find something every day (or at least weekly) that moves you forward.

⚡ Acknowledge the roadblocks that pop up, work through them, or revise your plan around them.

⚡ Pause to celebrate your progress and final destination. Don't just wait for the final end result; enjoy the progress points along the way.

A Few Final Words

This book has been a labor of love for me—love for those who are whip-smart with financial knowledge and choose to use and make others' lives better. Love for the financial industry. And love for every advisor I've had the honor to work with so far and those to come!

I am confident that strengthening your mind and skill set for selling efforts with the collaborative approach will benefit you. And, most importantly, it will help others choose to work with you!

And What's in it for **You**? Well for starters: stronger confidence, less stress, more income, growth, effective use of your hard-earned knowledge, and efficiency.

Wishing you the very best!

Dedicated to your success,

Nancy

Made in the USA
Las Vegas, NV
26 November 2024

12733873R00174